What Others Are Saying...

"There's good money to be made in foreclosures, and *Foreclosure Myths* shows you how to collect on it! Any new or experienced investor will find this book an invaluable resource guide that will eliminate hours of research and frustration."

—Tim Kleyla, President, The Mortgage House

"There has never been a better time for first-time homeowners and investors alike to jump into the market—and *Foreclosure Myths* gives them the ammo to do it right! Chip and Ralph have given people the blueprint they need to negotiate a win-win deal, and save thousands of hours and dollars! It's a must read."

—Steve Jacobson, President, Fairway Mortgage Corporation

"This is great! I've been looking for a book like this for a long time."

—Sonya Taylor, real estate investor

"Anyone looking for foreclosure answers can find them in this book! Having dealt with hundreds of properties and thousands of questions from borrowers and investors alike, I find this is the one resource that breaks it all down in an easy-to-follow format—and deals with the answers head-on!"

—Rocke Andrews, Loan Originator, Lending Arizona LLC;
   Education Chairman, National Association of Mortgage Brokers

"I wish I had had a copy of this book years ago when I got started investing—now I'll recommend a copy to every one of my clients!"

—Brad Kent, CEO, SmartLeads USA

"This should be on the bookshelf of anyone involved in real estate—or interested in getting into foreclosure properties."

—Ruth Faynor, national instructor and compliance expert

"What a great tool to take the fear out of foreclosure investing! I love the easy-to-follow format."

—Jonathon Combs, investment broker/REALTOR®

"Packed full of solid, useful information and tips for both new and experienced investors alike! When it comes to analyzing foreclosures, this book is easy to read and easy to follow, and makes it easy to succeed!"

—Tim Wooding, CMC, CRMS; CEO, Executive Mortgage Group

Foreclosure
Myths

Foreclosure Myths

77 Secrets to Making Money on Distressed Properties

RALPH R. ROBERTS   CHIP CUMMINGS

WILEY

John Wiley & Sons, Inc.

Published by John Wiley & Sons, Inc., Hoboken, New Jersey.
Published simultaneously in Canada.

Limit of Liability/Disclaimer of Warranty: While the publisher and author have used their best efforts in preparing this book, they make no representations or warranties with respect to the accuracy or completeness of the contents of this book and specifically disclaim any implied warranties of merchantability or fitness for a particular purpose. No warranty may be created or extended by sales representatives or written sales materials. The advice and strategies contained herein may not be suitable for your situation. You should consult with a professional where appropriate. Neither the publisher nor author shall be liable for any loss of profit or any other commercial damages, including but not limited to special, incidental, consequential, or other damages.

For general information on our other products and services or for technical support, please contact our Customer Care Department within the United States at (800) 762-2974, outside the United States at (317) 572-3993 or fax (317) 572-4002.

Wiley also publishes its books in a variety of electronic formats. Some content that appears in print may not be available in electronic books. For more information about Wiley products, visit our web site at www.wiley.com.

Library of Congress Cataloging-in-Publication Data:
Roberts, Ralph R., 1958–
  Foreclosure myths : 77 secrets to making money on distressed properties /
  Ralph R. Roberts, Chip Cummings.
    p. cm.
  Includes index.
  ISBN 978-0-470-28958-7 (pbk.)
  1. Real estate investment.   2. Foreclosure.   3. Residential real estate—
Purchasing.   I. Cummings, Chip.   II. Title.
  HD1382.5.R625 2008
  332.63'24—dc22   2008012122

Printed in the United States of America.

10 9 8 7 6 5 4 3 2 1

For Debbie Forth and Lois Maljak, our incredible personal assistants, who have helped us touch the lives of thousands of homebuyers over the years and have devoted countless hours to helping our customers—always with a smile!

To the millions of hardworking Americans who are pursuing the American Dream of Homeownership, building vibrant communities, and investing in the future of our great country, and to the thousands of loan officers, processors, underwriters, closers, real estate agents, and others who work hard every day to help people to do just that!

—Ralph & Chip

Important Disclosure Notice

This publication is designed to provide accurate and authoritative information with regard to the subject matter covered. It is sold with the understanding that the publisher, author, and individual contributors are not engaged in rendering professional services. If professional advice or other expert assistance is required, the services of a competent professional should be sought.

As with any type of printed material, information is subject to change. All reference items, web sites, addresses, phone numbers, and program requirements were current as of date of publishing, but may change from time to time. For current updated information and releases, go to www.TheForeclosureMyths.com.

Bulk quantities of this publication are available at a reduced cost for educational, non-profit, corporate, or association distribution. Contact the publisher toll-free at (866) 977-7900, or go to www.TheForeclosureMyths .com for more details.

Throughout this book, icons are used to illustrate important points—specific tips or strategies that can make, or cost, you thousands! They are:

 STOP! This message is a warning that, left unheeded, could wind up costing you extra time, money, or aggravation—or all three!

 GO! This message is a tip or strategy that can save you time, money, and probably a lot of headaches!

Contents

Foreword by Dr. Gary Lacefield   xv

Acknowledgments   xvii

About the Authors   xix

Introduction   xxi

1 Getting Started   1

MYTH #1   I'm Taking Unfair Advantage of Someone Else's
           Misfortune.   1
MYTH #2   Foreclosures Happen Only in "Bad"
           Neighborhoods and During Economic Downturns.   5
MYTH #3   Foreclosures Are Always the Result of Financial
           Irresponsibility.   7
MYTH #4   The Average Person Can't Find Foreclosures—You
           Have to Be an Insider.   9
MYTH #5   I Need a Lot of Money to Get Started.   10
MYTH #6   If Foreclosure Rates Are Rising, Buying Doesn't
           Make Sense Because There Are Too Many Homes
           Already on the Market.   11
MYTH #7   The Process Is Incredibly Time Consuming; There's
           No Way to Get Started If I Already Have a
           Full-Time Job.   13
MYTH #8   I Have to Be an Expert.   15
MYTH #9   Real Estate Agents Won't Help Me with
           Foreclosures—There's Nothing in It for Them.   16
MYTH #10   I Can Do This by Myself.   19

2   The Foreclosure Process   23

MYTH # 11	The Process Takes a Long Time.	24
MYTH # 12	I Can't Get It—It's in Bankruptcy.	26
MYTH # 13	I Can't Help Out the Homeowner.	27
MYTH # 14	They'll Save the Property, and I'll Be Out My Time and Money.	30
MYTH # 15	They Can Still Cancel the Sale.	31
MYTH # 16	I Have to Wait Until It's Listed with a Real Estate Agent.	32
MYTH # 17	It Was Published in the Paper, So I Can Buy It Now.	33
MYTH # 18	I Have to Wait Until the Auction to Buy the Property.	34
MYTH # 19	If I'm Not the High Bidder at Auction, I Can Forget Buying the House.	37

3   Finding the "Right" Properties   41

MYTH # 20	Every Foreclosure Is a Good Deal.	42
MYTH # 21	I'm Buying a Home at the Foreclosure Auction.	45
MYTH # 22	Courthouse Auctions Are the Only Source of Foreclosure Properties.	47
MYTH # 23	Real Estate Agents Always Have First Crack at the Good Deals.	50
MYTH # 24	I Can Find Better Deals Outside My Own Area.	51
MYTH # 25	Foreclosed Properties Are Always Trashed and Need Extensive and Costly Repairs.	53
MYTH # 26	Something Else Is Wrong with the Property If It Was in Foreclosure.	55
MYTH # 27	I Don't Need an Inspection.	56
MYTH # 28	I Can't Get Inside, So There's No Way for Me to Estimate the Property Value.	58
MYTH # 29	Never Bid on a Second Mortgage.	60

4 Analyzing the Deal 63

MYTH #**30** I Found the Opportunity Too Late—There's Not Enough Time. 63

MYTH #**31** I Found the Opportunity Too Early—I'll Probably Waste My Time. 65

MYTH #**32** I Can't Get a Good Deal Through a Real Estate Agent. 66

MYTH #**33** I Can't Get a Good Deal from Bankruptcy. 68

MYTH #**34** I Can't Get a Good Deal on a Government REO. 70

MYTH #**35** I Can't Get a Good Deal from the Lender. 73

MYTH #**36** The Purchase Price and My Fix-Up Costs Are the Only Costs I Need to Consider. 77

MYTH #**37** I Should Adjust My Bidding Strategy Depending on How Many Bidders Show Up and How Eager They Seem to Be to Purchase the Property. 80

MYTH #**38** It Doesn't Matter Where It's Located; Since I'll Pay Well Below Market Value, the Location Isn't Important. 82

MYTH #**39** I Shouldn't Bring in Experts to Help Me Analyze the Deal; the Fewer People Who Know It's Available, the Better. 85

5 Financing the Property 87

MYTH #**40** Interest on Loans from Private Investors Is Too High. 87

MYTH #**41** Lenders Don't Want to Deal with Little Ole Me. 90

MYTH #**42** Lenders Won't Be Willing to Talk to Me Until I Have a Deal on the Table. 91

MYTH #**43** I Should Use as Much of My *Own* Money as Possible. 93

MYTH #**44** I Can't Use FHA or VA Financing. 94

MYTH #**45** I Can't Use a Home Equity Loan to Finance the Property, Since I Don't Own the Property Yet. 95

MYTH #**46** Since the Property Is Already in Foreclosure, I Can't
Assume the Owner's Loan. 97
MYTH #**47** The Property Has to Be in Good Shape to Get
Financing. 99
MYTH #**48** Taking on a Partner Will Merely Cut into My
Profits. 101

6 **Securing the Property** **103**

MYTH #**49** Once I Purchase the Property at Auction,
I Can Take Immediate Possession. 103
MYTH #**50** Only Real Estate Pros Are Allowed to Attend Real
Estate Auctions. 106
MYTH #**51** There Will Be Lots of People Bidding against Me. 107
MYTH #**52** The Higher the Bidding Goes, and the
More People Bidding, the More Likely It's a
Great Property. 108
MYTH #**53** I Won't Be Able to Get Good Title to the Property. 110
MYTH #**54** I'll Have to Pay the Back Taxes and Insurance. 113
MYTH #**55** I Can't Force the Previous Owners to Vacate the
Property. 114
MYTH #**56** I Don't Need Insurance Until the Previous
Owners Move Out and I Take Possession of
the Property. 116

7 **Cashing In!** **119**

MYTH #**57** I Need to Finish Renovations Before I Sell. 119
MYTH #**58** The More I Put into a Property, the More
Return I'll Get. 121
MYTH #**59** I'll Save Money and Make More Profit If
I Make All Repairs and Upgrades
Myself. 126

MYTH #**60** I Can't Make a Profit. 128

MYTH #**61** I Won't Be Able to Sell It—They Couldn't! 129

MYTH #**62** I Already Have a Home; My Best Bet Is to Flip the Foreclosures I Purchase. 132

MYTH #**63** The Property Will Be Easiest to Flip When It's Market Ready. 134

MYTH #**64** It's a Foreclosure; I'll Still Make a $10,000 Profit! 135

MYTH #**65** I Should Feel Guilty. 137

8 Avoiding Disaster 141

MYTH #**66** I'm an Experienced Real Estate Investor, So I Don't Need to Do My Homework. 141

MYTH #**67** I Am Familiar with the House, So I Don't Need to Inspect It. 142

MYTH #**68** The House Looks Great—It Won't Need Many Repairs! 144

MYTH #**69** This House Is Amazing—It's Worth a Fortune! 145

MYTH #**70** I Can Trust What the Homeowners Tell Me. 149

MYTH #**71** If I Find Myself in Financial Difficulty, I'll Never Escape Foreclosure. 150

MYTH #**72** I'll Be Able to Flip This House in a Couple of Weeks! 155

MYTH #**73** If I Make Some Repairs Before I Take Possession of the Property, I'll Save Valuable Time. 156

MYTH #**74** It's a Stretch, but I Think I Can Make an Extra $10,000 on This Property. 158

MYTH #**75** I'm Making Good Money on Real Estate, but I Should Keep My Day Job. 161

MYTH #**76** I've Put So Much Time into This Deal—I Refuse to Let Anyone Outbid Me! 162

MYTH #**77** Foreclosure Investing Is Just Too Complicated—I Can't Do It. 163

Appendix   **165**

Resources   165
Sample Forms & Checklists   166
State Foreclosure Guidelines   171

Index   **189**

Foreword

Unfortunately for many, the great American dream of home ownership has turned into a nightmare. As I write this, foreclosures are occurring in epidemic proportions in many areas all across the United States. Bad financial decisions, predatory lending, and a soft economy have converged to create the perfect storm in the housing industry, and many families are paying the price.

Almost every cloud in the housing market, however, has a silver lining. With foreclosures on the rise, property values, which had surged during the late 1990s and early in the new millennium, have taken a nosedive, and many homeowners and real estate investors who thought they would never have the opportunity to buy real estate at a reasonable price are now finding it a much more affordable option. After all, if you make money by buying low and selling high, then you need market downturns to buy low.

One of the best ways to buy low in today's housing market is to buy property in foreclosure or pre-foreclosure—properties often described as *distressed.* And you don't have to be an investor to cash in on these bargains. Anyone can benefit—individuals, couples looking for their first home, families looking to scale up or scale down, even retirees whose fixed incomes have made everything less affordable.

Average consumers and even some seasoned real estate investors, however, don't know how to find the best deals. They don't know how to research properties to make sure they're not getting a bum deal. Many don't even realize that what they are bidding on at a foreclosure auction is not a property but a mortgage—and some who bid on the wrong mortgage have learned the hard way that this is an all-too-easy way to lose a lot of money.

Fortunately, *Foreclosure Myths: 77 Secrets to Making Money on Distressed Properties* pulls the veil back on the mysterious world of foreclosure investing. Seasoned REALTOR® and foreclosure investor Ralph

R. Roberts together with investor and mortgage veteran Chip Cummings tear down the 77 most common myths that often discourage consumers from investing in foreclosures. In the process, they provide plenty of how-to information showing consumers and investors how to locate the best deals and purchase properties before (pre-foreclosures), during (foreclosure auctions), and after (bank-owned properties) foreclosure. They also show you how to perform your due diligence after the purchase to ensure that you don't lose the property to another investor.

Having been in the real estate industry for almost three decades as a compliance officer, an industry expert, and a federal regulator, I thought I knew almost everything worth knowing about foreclosures. After having the opportunity to read the manuscript for this book, I can state, unequivocally, that I now know everything that is worth knowing about foreclosures. By reading this book, so will you.

I believe that knowledge is power. The knowledge you will acquire by reading this book will empower you to invest with confidence. As an added bonus, much of the information that Ralph and Chip reveal will also help you avoid the foreclosure trap. This book is your key to the American dream of home ownership!

—Dr. Gary Lacefield
President, Risk Mitigation Group

Acknowledgments

Every book demands a group effort, and many individuals and organizations assisted us during this project, but we offer special thanks to our dedicated staff at Northwind Financial Corporation, Chip Cummings Unlimited!, and Roberts Realty, especially our personal assistants, Debbie Forth and Lois Maljak, who keep us in line.

Special thanks also go to our acquisitions editor, Shannon Vargo, and the rest of the John Wiley & Sons team who made things happen, kept the project on track, and ensured the production of a high-quality product. Editors Linda Indig, Kim Dayman, and Jessica Langan-Peck deserve a special round of applause for making our jobs fun in addition to treating our work with such care. Thanks also to our agent, Neil Salkind of Studio B, without whom this book and others would never have launched. Separately, our editor Jeff Haden deserves a great deal of praise for spending the extra time in making us look and sound so good!

We also wish to express our appreciation to the many associations and organizations who contributed, including:

National Association of Mortgage Brokers
Mortgage Bankers Association
National Association of REALTORS®
Michigan Mortgage Brokers Association
RealtyTrac
Fannie Mae
Freddie Mac
U.S. Department of Housing and Urban Development
U.S. Department of Veterans Affairs

Many different real estate agents, loan officers, mortgage originators, investors, and foreclosure attorneys also contributed their experiences—and continue to contribute their expertise to our industry on a daily basis by doing it the right way!

And last, but not least, thanks to our families, who put up with some long days and even longer nights and still seem to smile when we tell them, "We have another deal!" Their patience and willingness to allow us to have fun with what we do on a daily basis gives us the energy to make a difference in the lives of so many people out there. Bless you all.

About the Authors

Ralph Roberts, CRS, GRI

Ralph R. Roberts is the official spokesman for Guthy-Renker Home, a company dedicated to equipping home buyers, sellers, and real estate professionals with the tools, information, and community setting they need to achieve mutual success. Visit www.HurryHome.com and www.RealtyTracker.com to experience the exciting innovations that Guthy-Renker Home offers now and is planning for the future.

Ralph has been profiled by the Associated Press, CNN, and *Time* magazine, and has done hundreds of radio interviews. He is a seasoned professional in all areas of real estate, including buying and selling homes, investing in real estate, and building and managing real estate agent teams. He is co-author of *Mortgage Myths: 77 Secrets That Will Save You Thousands on Home Financing* (John Wiley & Sons), and has written several other successful books, including *Sell It Yourself: Sell Your Home Faster and for More Money without Using a Broker* (Adams Media Corporation); *Walk Like a Giant, Sell Like a Madman: America's #1 Salesman Shows You How to Sell Anything* (Collins); *52 Weeks of Sales Success: America's #1 Salesman Shows You How to Close Every Deal!* (Collins); *Real Wealth by Investing in Real Estate* (Prentice Hall); *Protect Yourself Against Real Estate and Mortgage Fraud: Preserving the American Dream of Home-ownership* (Kaplan); *Flipping Houses for Dummies* (John Wiley & Sons); *Foreclosure Investing for Dummies* (John Wiley & Sons); and *Advanced Selling for Dummies* (John Wiley & Sons).

To find out more about Ralph Roberts and what he can offer you and your organization as a speaker and coach, visit AboutRalph.com. For details on how to protect yourself and your home from real estate and mortgage fraud, check out Ralph's blog at FlippingFrenzy.com. And don't miss the latest addition to Ralph's family of web sites and blogs,

GetFlipping.com, where Ralph offers additional information and tips on the art of flipping houses. You can contact Ralph by e-mailing him at RalphRoberts@RalphRoberts.com or calling 586-751-0000.

Chip Cummings, CMC

Chip Cummings is a recognized expert in the areas of real estate lending and e-marketing, and a Certified Mortgage Consultant with over 24 years in the mortgage industry and over a billion dollars in sales volume. He is an experienced real estate investor in both residential and commercial properties, and bought his first foreclosure at the age of 19.

Chip has written hundreds of articles and appeared numerous times on radio and television with FOX News, NBC, ABC, and the *Neil Cavuto Show*, and in various magazines, including *Entrepreneur, Mortgage Originator, Real Estate Banker/Broker*, and *The Mortgage Press*. An experienced professional in all areas of real estate financing and investing, including residential and commercial mortgages, government lending, regulatory and compliance issues, he is past president of the Michigan Mortgage Brokers Association (MMBA), and is a licensed mortgage lender in Michigan.

As an international speaker, he has addressed groups and organizations of all types, and trains thousands of mortgage professionals from around the country every year. Chip is a certified national trainer for continuing education in over 40 states, and has served as an expert witness in state and federal courts. He is also co-author of *Mortgage Myths: 77 Secrets That Will Save You Thousands on Home Financing* (John Wiley & Sons), and author of *ABC's of FHA Lending* (Northwind) and *Stop Selling and Start Listening! Marketing Strategies That Create Top Producers* (Northwind).

Chip lives in Rockford, Michigan, with his wife Lisa and three children, Katelyn, CJ, and Joe.

To learn more about Chip Cummings, his many success products, or how he can help your organization as a speaker or business consultant, visit www.ChipCummings.com. To receive a complimentary subscription to his muitimedia e-newsletter "The Marketing Minute," check out www.TheMarketingMinute.com, or www.eCoachingClub.com. You can also reach Chip by e-mailing him at info@ChipCummings.com or by calling 616-977-7900.

Introduction

Ralph Roberts

Although foreclosure can be devastating to the people who lose their homes, foreclosure offers excellent opportunities for others to scoop up properties at bargain prices—often 20% or more below the property's true market value. Because of this, many real estate investors specialize in foreclosures and have earned handsome profits by doing so.

Because you have picked up this book, I think I can safely assume that you have been thinking of buying a foreclosure property yourself.

So, what's stopping you?

I would guess that one of two things is holding you back. Either you fear that you don't yet know enough about investing in foreclosures, or you have a mistaken belief that foreclosure investing is far too risky.

This initial fear is good. It prevents you from diving in ill-prepared. I have seen dozens of novice investors who've spent a day at a foreclosure investment seminar get seriously burned at their first auction by bidding on (and buying) second mortgages and getting stuck with what ultimately became worthless pieces of paper. One investor I met lost about $100,000 in a single afternoon!

Yes, foreclosure investing is risky. No guaranteed profits are to be had, and you can certainly lose money, but every venture that is potentially profitable carries some risk. In this book, Chip and I help you put the potential profitability and risks of foreclosure investing in the proper perspective as we blast away at the 77 most common foreclosure myths. Throughout this book, we provide you with the tools and techniques to minimize your risks while maximizing your potential profitability.

Chip Cummings

Sometimes, bad things happen to good people. Unfortunately, many people get into situations that are beyond their means, or beyond their control—especially when it comes to owning real estate.

But this can also open up some incredible opportunities for you—opportunities to purchase your first home at a great savings; the opportunity to pick up good investment properties at a bargain; and even the opportunity to help people who are down on their luck.

As an investor, I've owned lots of properties—many of them foreclosures. And the best deals are usually (no, make that *always*) the ones that are win-win for everyone involved. Likewise, in the mortgage arena, I've helped countless people get into their first home or investment property, and in the process saved many a seller's credit, equity, and sometimes dignity in the process. And you can, too.

In *Foreclosure Myths*, Ralph and I have set out to put an end to the many misconceptions people have about the foreclosure process, the players involved, and how to make sure you can structure each deal as a win-win transaction. Whether you're a first-timer or a seasoned veteran, knowing and understanding the myths that we've uncovered through years of experience will save you hours of time, thousands of dollars, and a truckload of heartaches!

Foreclosure properties are abundant in the marketplace. You didn't cause it, but you can certainly use it to your advantage, and get into your first home or start accumulating some great investment properties. Either way, we're glad to have the opportunity to guide you down the path and help you avoid the land mines known as the *Foreclosure Myths*!

August 2008

Getting Started

Every investor knows the secret to earning profits—buy low and sell high. In the real estate market, however, buying low can be a real challenge, particularly when home values are on the rise. Foreclosures are one exception. When homeowners can no longer afford to make their monthly mortgage payments, for whatever reason, they either have to sell and settle with the lender or face losing their home at auction. Either way, the homeowner is at a distinct disadvantage at the bargaining table, giving you, the investor, more power in picking up the property for less than it's worth.

MYTH # **1**

I'm Taking Unfair Advantage of Someone Else's Misfortune.

Fact: You Could Be Saving Their Financial Lives

Thinking of buying a property that's in foreclosure may cause you to feel like you're kicking someone when they're down. This doesn't have to be the case. While the circumstances are unfortunate for the homeowners, you, as an investor, can provide the homeowners with a graceful exit: Unless the homeowners can secure the funds to bring the mortgage current—which is called *reinstating* the mortgage—or work out some other deal with their lender, they will lose their home. It's that simple, and it's not your fault. (But you may be able to help them make a bad situation better, as you'll see in a later Myth!)

Are you still not convinced? Then let's take a close look at mortgage loans and foreclosures.

The foreclosure process isn't as mysterious as it may seem. Due to federal and state laws, lenders must follow a specific process in order to foreclose on a property. (Understanding the process flow will also help you find investment opportunities, so take the time to read this closely.)

Let's first look at what happens when a lender is allowed to foreclose. The process starts with the mortgage itself. A mortgage creates five covenants (a *covenant* is basically a promise):

1. The homeowner promises to repay the debt.
2. The homeowner will insure the building against fire or damage to protect the lender's interest in the property.
3. The building or dwelling cannot be demolished or removed without the consent of the lender.
4. The entire principal will become due in the event that the borrower defaults on the payment of principal, interest, taxes, or assessments.
5. The lender will consent to the appointment of a receiver in the event of foreclosure.

The first three items are agreements the homeowner must adhere to. If those covenants are breached, the lender bank must pursue items 4 and 5. (Why the word *must*? Because banks are really *trust officers*: They aren't loaning their own money; they're loaning money that belongs to depositors or investors. They don't have the right to take risks with other people's money, so they must follow these covenants.)

The last two covenants give the bank the means to foreclose. One provides for the appointment of a receiver—typically a lawyer—who conducts the sale of the property. The other allows the bank to accelerate payments and ask for the entire balance. If the bank's lawyers take a homeowner to court, they want all of the money, and if it can't be paid, they want a judgment against the homeowner. In simple terms, the bank wants out of the deal because the homeowner has not lived up to his or her obligations.

It's important to note that until a judgment has been obtained, the homeowner is not truly under threat of foreclosure. Once the judgment is obtained, the lender can take action to sell the property or its interest in the property, and eventually have the homeowner evicted, unless he or she moves out voluntarily.

After a judgment has been handed down against the homeowner, a time is set for the public sale of the property at auction. If the homeowner can't come up with the entire amount of the judgment award before the sale, that's it: No more delays, no more compromises—the sale will be held. Often these sales are held at the county courthouse, and in many cases are actually held on the courthouse steps. The auctions have to be publicized, are open to the public, and anyone may attend.

The court then appoints a receiver—again, typically a lawyer—to conduct the sale of the homeowner's property. Ordinarily, real property can't be transferred without both parties in the purchase agreement signing the transfer deed. Since the homeowner is unlikely to voluntarily sign away his or her home, the receiver has the legal authority to sign a valid deed (often called a *sheriff's deed*) transferring the ownership to a new purchaser.

Now that you understand the process, let's look at the different stages of foreclosure. We'll pretend you're the homeowner facing financial difficulties.

If you've missed a payment, most lenders will call to remind you that the payment was due and attempt to arrange payment. (You may receive a number of calls if you continue to fail to make your payment.) As a result of their calls, you may enter into a *deferred payment plan*, or what's called a *workout*. If the calls (or workout plan) aren't successful, typically the lender will then send a letter documenting the missed payment(s) and requesting immediate payment of the past-due amount. Once you've missed several payments, the lender's lawyer will send you a strongly worded "last chance" letter. Receiving a letter from the lawyer means you're in trouble; you haven't just committed an oversight that the bank wants corrected, but you are now considered a serious "problem debtor." When you hear from the lawyer, it means the bank has committed resources (time and money) to get you to pay on time—they're serious.

If you can't reach an agreement with the lender or lawyer, you'll be served with a summons. (The lawyer has very little reason to negotiate at this point, so normally the only "agreement" you'll be able to reach is that you'll make your loan payments on time—starting immediately.)

After *service*, which is the process by which you're physically presented with the summons, the attorney will also file papers with the county courthouse. All other individuals with claims against the property—they're called *junior* obligations—such as second mortgages, home improvement loans, judgments, or other liens, are also served with papers, so they have the right to try to protect their interests as well. (It's important to note that if the foreclosing party is negligent in notifying junior lien holders, those creditors have a valid claim for repayment against the eventual new owner of the property. That's why purchasing title insurance when buying foreclosure properties is absolutely essential: You protect yourself against subsequent claims you didn't know about. After all, you don't want to be responsible for a lack of attention to detail by the foreclosing party!)

To enforce money judgments, the lender also must serve you personally. That's one reason foreclosure actions can take so long—the homeowner(s) must be tracked down and physically handed the summons by a process server or court agent. Often the homeowners won't want to be served and will do their best to avoid the server!

Each jurisdiction has different laws and rules, but generally speaking, if a person can't be located and all "reasonable" efforts have been made to find them, a procedure for publication is put into place. This typically consists of a public notice printed in the classified section of one or more local newspapers.

Most jurisdictions also require public notice regardless of whether the homeowner has been served. This allows parties with a legitimate claim to come forward to protect their interests. (To determine the specific process in your area, refer to the Appendix in the back of this book, or call your local city or county offices.)

After the publication process is complete, the foreclosure action will proceed. If you can't come to an agreement with the bank's lawyer and can't come up with the funds to pay off the loan, your property will be sold at a foreclosure auction and you'll eventually be evicted from the property (if you haven't already left).

Later on, we'll look at purchasing properties during pre-foreclosure, which can be a financial lifesaver for a desperate homeowner. But, if you purchase a property at a foreclosure auction, you're not the one responsible for the homeowner's loss. The foreclosure ship has already sailed. *Someone* will purchase the property—and if it's a great investment, that someone might as well be you.

 Whether you buy a home at auction or purchase directly from the homeowners in pre-foreclosure, always treat the homeowners with empathy and a sense of fairness while still working to earn a reasonable profit. In addition to making you and the homeowners feel better about what happened, demonstrating compassion will improve your reputation in the area and help convince other distressed homeowners to call you instead of someone else when they need to sell their home in foreclosure.

MYTH # **2**

Foreclosures Happen Only in "Bad" Neighborhoods and During Economic Downturns.

Fact: Foreclosures Happen Every Day, in Every City in the United States

As we write this, rising foreclosure rates are all over the news. (In fact, Chip has spent a significant amount of time appearing on news broadcasts discussing the lending crisis and the ramifications for homeowners.) The number of properties entering some stage of foreclosure in 2007 increased in 86 of the nation's 100 largest metro areas over 2006 levels. In California, where home values had more than tripled since 1995, plunging home prices and tighter lending standards cooled off the market and left many financially strapped homeowners—some facing steep payment hikes from adjustable rate mortgages—with limited options to save their homes. And the numbers keep going up. (See Figure 1.1.)

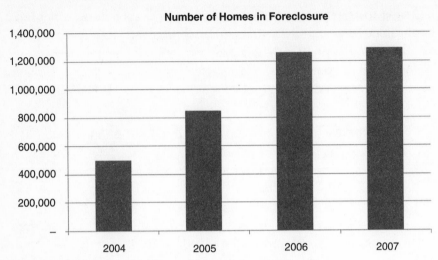

Figure 1.1 Yearly Number of Properties in Foreclosure
Source: RealtyTrac.com.

Foreclosures can occur anywhere, and in any neighborhood, due to any number of causes. For example, studies show that a loan's default risk is directly tied to the size of the down payment: The lower the down payment, the greater the likelihood of default—and low down payments can be made on any property, regardless of value. In cases where higher down payments were originally made, low interest rates make home equity loan advances and cash-out refinancing appealing, and allow homeowners to take out cash generated from down payments and from appreciation. The Census Bureau estimated that in 2004 approximately $569 billion in home equity was extracted through refinancing, taking out second mortgages, or simply extracting cash during a move. The less equity remaining in a home, the less cushion the homeowners have, and the higher the likelihood of default. When cash-out extractions rise, more homeowners are at risk.

Liberal lending standards also led some consumers to borrow more than they could afford: Census Bureau statistics show that the average household spends almost a third of their income on housing costs, up from about 20% in 2000. As a result, financial difficulties such as a job loss, unexpected medical costs, or other emergencies quickly put a homeowner's mortgage in jeopardy. Rising consumer debt burden means any disruption in financial circumstances like lost income, illness, or divorce can seriously impact a homeowner's ability to make payments—no matter where they live.

We'll look at some of the reasons why foreclosures occur in the next Myth. (We'll be brief, because a detailed analysis of the causes of foreclosure could fill an entire book!) Just keep in mind that foreclosure rates have, over a long period of time, remained relatively stable. Even at its lowest levels over the last 50 years, the foreclosure rate has remained above .5%.

While "bad" neighborhoods have their share of foreclosures, you can also find multimillion-dollar properties for sale at foreclosure auctions; if the homeowners cannot meet their obligations, foreclosure may occur. While it's true that economic downturns do tend to cause foreclosure rates to increase, every day, in every city and county in the United States, homes are foreclosed on. This opens the door for you!

Avoid the temptation to buy into an area with plenty of foreclosure opportunities just because finding foreclosures is easier. In areas where foreclosures are rampant, you may have more trouble selling or leasing the property later, and the property may not appreciate in value as quickly. Ideally, you want to find the hidden gem—a foreclosure property in a popular area.

MYTH # **3**

Foreclosures Are Always the Result of Financial Irresponsibility.

Fact: Unforeseen Events Can Derail the Best of Financial Plans

If a family loses their home in foreclosure, it's easy to assume they were irresponsible or got in over their "financial heads." Despite the fact that those are possible reasons for foreclosure, many times foreclosure is out of the homeowner's control. Defaulting on a loan could also have been caused by any of the following:

- **Divorce:** Approximately half of all marriages end in divorce. Who keeps the house and who pays for the house—and whether the house is even affordable any longer—can be a major issue. Unfortunately, in many instances, pure spite takes over and common sense disappears! (In fact, the cost of the divorce itself can even be the main cause of foreclosure.)
- **Health problems:** Unexpected illnesses or injuries can cost thousands in medical bills, and the rising rate of uninsured Americans leaves fewer people with a safety net. When a medical emergency occurs, mortgage payments are sometimes understandably seen as less important, at least in the short term.
- **Job loss:** Losing a job is a common cause of foreclosure. As unemployment rates increase, foreclosure rates naturally tend to rise. But even during booming economic times, some companies lay off employees, transfer or consolidate, or just plain go out of business.
- **Predatory lending:** Irresponsible, greedy, or poorly trained loan originators can sell a homeowner on a loan that sets the homeowner up for failure. Prior to the mortgage meltdown that started in 2007, this was a common problem.
- **Soaring cost of living:** When pay increases fail to keep up with inflation, homeowners may not be able to maintain their lifestyle. We have seen sudden increases in property taxes, insurance premiums, and fuel costs without comparable increases in personal income.
- **Death:** If the sole wage earner dies, the likelihood increases that the family will lose their home in foreclosure.
- **Taxes:** Some mortgage programs do not include tax escrow accounts, and it becomes easy for a homeowner to fall behind. In these cases, the lender can call the loan due and accelerate payments to avoid a tax-lien sale.

While financial irresponsibility is a common cause, as you can see, death, job loss, medical expenses, and divorce are also common triggers for a property foreclosure. Sadly, bad things do happen to well-meaning, financially responsible people.

When dealing with homeowners in foreclosure, avoid making judgments or placing blame. What's past is past. The homeowners need to focus on the present and their future instead of beating themselves up or blaming others for their misfortune.

MYTH # **4**

The Average Person Can't Find Foreclosures—You Have to Be an Insider.

Fact: Foreclosures Are Public Knowledge; You Just Have to Know Where to Look

By law, foreclosure is a public process. If the homeowners have not shown a commitment to bring the loan current, the lender will initiate formal foreclosure proceedings. Their attorney will post a foreclosure notice, sometimes called a *Notice of Default*, and the foreclosure will be officially underway.

And again, it's public—these notices must be published in the local newspaper. (If your locality has multiple newspapers, at least one will be considered the *paper of record* where Notices are always posted. Call your local courthouse to identify where postings are published.) You can also visit your locality's Register of Deeds and view current foreclosure notices. While you're there, ask if you can get on their mailing list if they have one. Many areas will mail or e-mail notices on a weekly or periodic basis, often for no charge.

Here's a quick tip: Don't bother subscribing to commercial foreclosure services. (The Internet is full of them.) There is simply no valid reason to pay a premium for information you can receive for free (and those "exclusive" leads you get on the Internet are usually outdated). Besides, tracking notices in your local newspaper or by visiting the courthouse will help you keep your finger on the pulse of your local real estate market. The only way you can gain "insider" knowledge is by paying close attention to your market and by building a network of real estate professionals and investors in your area.

You can become somewhat of an *insider* by earning a good track record of dealing fairly with distressed homeowners and by networking with people who commonly assist homeowners in foreclosure, including real estate agents, bankers, bankruptcy attorneys, foreclosure attorneys, divorce attorneys, and credit counselors.

MYTH # **5**

I Need a Lot of Money to Get Started.

Fact: With the Right Preparation, You Can Purchase Foreclosures with Very Little Cash of Your Own

Let's be clear: When you buy a foreclosed property, you *will* need cash. It just doesn't all have to be *your* cash.

To buy a property at auction, you'll need to bring a cashier's check with you. The amount varies based on your area and the opening bid. While some localities require a check for the full purchase price, it's more common for the standard to be along the lines of 10% of the purchase price or $10,000, whichever is greater. Then you'll typically have up to 30 days to come up with the remainder of the purchase price; in some areas, you'll have only a few days or hours. (The terms and conditions of the sale will be included in the printed foreclosure notice, or you can call the courthouse for locality-specific information.)

How do you know how large a cashier's check you'll need? It's easy. First determine the maximum you're willing to pay for the property, or your *walk-away price*. Make a solemn pledge to yourself that no matter what happens during the auction, you will not bid one penny more than this amount. If your maximum price is $150,000 and you need 10% of the purchase price at time of auction, you'll need a cashier's check for $15,000. Simply have your bank (or lender) make out the check in your name, and if you win the bidding, endorse the check over to the locality.

You'll need funds for other purposes, too. We'll look at financing more closely later on, but for now remember you'll need funds to cover the purchase price of the property; any up-front loan costs; holding costs like insurance, taxes, utilities, and loan payments; the cost of repairs and renovations; and even closing costs if you sell the property.

Does this sound like a lot? In some cases it can be, but your goal should be to leverage the power of *other people's money* (OPM). By limiting the amount of cash you put in and maximizing the value of money you borrow, you may share some of your profits with your lenders, but you'll lower your risk and increase the rate of return on your investment.

Here's the bottom line: If you find a property with good investment potential, by doing a little homework you can find sources of cash to help you make that investment, even if you have very little money of your own. For more about borrowing money, check out our other Myths book—*Mortgage Myths: 77 Secrets That Will Save You Thousands on Home Financing* (John Wiley & Sons, 2008).

Always check the bidding and deposit requirements first! You may be able to simply supply a bank Letter of Credit, or you may have to come up with the entire amount!

If possible, convince the lender to accept the value of the foreclosure property as the sole collateral for the loan. This way, if something does go wrong, your lender will have less power to seize your personal assets in lieu of payment.

MYTH # **6**

If Foreclosure Rates Are Rising, Buying Doesn't Make Sense Because There Are Too Many Homes Already on the Market.

Fact: Everyone Has to Live Somewhere and Buyers Are Always Interested in the Right Properties

From an investment point of view, your main concern (in fact, when you get down to it, your *only* concern) is whether a potential deal makes good financial sense. So, let's say foreclosure rates have risen sharply and there is a glut of homes on the market in your area. Should you buy a property at foreclosure?

No matter where you live, what the economic conditions are, and what the real estate market is like, the answer is the same: *It depends.*

Is this a copout? Not at all: You shouldn't make a decision on *any* investment without analyzing the risks, rewards, and potential involved. Remember, you're not doing this for fun; you're doing it to get a return on your time and investment!

Say you live in an area where foreclosure rates are incredibly high and every real estate agent in town says it's a buyer's market—the supply of homes is much greater than the demand. As a result, home prices have fallen, especially on high-end properties.

Then you find a three-bedroom brick ranch in foreclosure in a good neighborhood. The other houses are well maintained, crime rates are low, and the schools have a good reputation. In the last month, three similar houses sold for $175,000. You are willing to pay $100,000 for the foreclosure property—that's your walk-away price—and you esti-mate you'll spend $10,000 on cosmetic repairs. Then you plan to flip it, and to make sure it sells quickly, you'll price it at $165,000, which is slightly below fair market value. Even after holding costs, you estimate you'll make approximately $30,000 to $40,000 in profit. Is that a good deal?

Based on the information presented here, the answer is yes, even though foreclosure rates are rising. The risk is relatively low, the return is relatively high, and you feel good about the possibilities for a quick resale based on your pricing strategy.

At the same time, don't let your desire for quick profits blind you to economic realities. Rising foreclosure rates tend to cause home values to fall, or at least stay flat. If your walk-away price for the same house is significantly higher, and you assume you'll need to sell the house for $185,000 in order to make a small profit, the deal no longer makes sense because the likelihood of selling for a premium over fair market value is very small.

No matter what the market, do your homework. Realistically assess the property's value, the cost of holding and fixing up the property, and your eventual sales price, and then determine whether the deal makes good financial sense. No deal is a sure winner or loser: The answer to the question "Is this a good deal?" should always be, "It depends," at least until after you've done your homework!

 When you're doing your homework, also explore what's happening with rental properties in your area. People still need a place to live, and as long as the area is not seeing a mass exodus, residents are probably renting rather than buying. Instead of flipping the property (selling soon after buying), consider shifting to a buy-and-hold strategy and leasing the property out at least until the market turns around. (As demand for rental properties increases, so do rents.)

MYTH # **7**

The Process Is Incredibly Time Consuming; There's No Way to Get Started If I Already Have a Full-Time Job.

Fact: Most Real Estate Investors Have Full-Time Jobs

Real estate offers a variety of moneymaking opportunities and is a finite commodity; as the old saying goes, "No one's making new land." You can purchase your own home and watch it grow in value, you can find an undervalued foreclosure property and flip it for a quick profit, or you can purchase properties to rent to others, letting them make your mortgage payments for you.

And the beauty of real estate investing is that you *can* do it part time. Look around you. Most people who own residential rental properties do so "on the side." We know a dentist who owns 12 rental properties, 8 of which he bought at foreclosure. Others buy one property at a time to repair, renovate, and then flip, doing some of the work themselves at night or on the weekends and hiring friends or contractors to perform any necessary skilled labor. Still others create partnerships: One partner finds and evaluates the deals and lines up funding and financing, while the other takes care of the repairs and renovations.

In fact, finding a partner or partners is a great way to spread the workload and at the same time minimize each partner's risk. (And working as a team can be a lot of fun!)

To get your feet wet and gain experience without incurring any risk, make a few practice runs. Find foreclosure notices and check out the properties in person. Just remember to stay on the street and off the actual property—walking onto the property uninvited can be considered trespassing. Try to determine what your walk-away price would be.

Then attend the auction and see how the process works. In fact, we feel you should never attend an auction with the intention of bidding before you have gone to at least five auctions as an observer.

Pay attention to the bidding. After a few auctions, you'll be able to tell which bidders give in to buyer's frenzy (we call them amateurs!). You'll also start to see some of the same faces, and you'll quickly learn who the regulars are. Not only will that give you a sense of who the serious bidders are, but you may be able to strike up a partnership with another real estate investor. The more experience you can gain, even just by watching and mentally practicing, the more comfortable you'll be when you enter the process for real.

If you already have a full-time job, you're under no pressure to make a living from real estate investing. You can move at your own pace and your own comfort level. And if your comfort level is currently low, check out Myth #10 for ways to decrease your apprehension and increase your chances for success!

If you do decide to partner with another investor, be as careful in choosing your new partner as you are when choosing a mate. This doesn't necessarily mean that your partnership will be without problems (after all, half of all marriages in the United States end in divorce), but it will decrease your chances of taking on a partner who's committed to ripping you off.

MYTH # **8**

I Have to Be an Expert.

Fact: The Foreclosure Process Is Simple to Understand: You Don't Have to Be an Authority, But You Do Have to Be Willing to Put in the Effort

If you've ever purchased a home, you have a sense of how real estate financing and transactions work. (In fact, if you don't currently live in your own home, unless you plan to purchase a property at foreclosure to live in, get a copy of our book *Mortgage Myths: 77 Secrets That Will Save You Thousands on Home Financing* and focus on owning your own home first before investing in other properties.) Reading foreclosure notices, attending auctions, and repairing and flipping homes is not rocket science. Thousands of Americans do so every year without specialized knowledge or training. Some people buy and sell dozens of properties each year; the only difference between you and those investors is experience and *effort*—and before they bought their first foreclosure property, they didn't have experience either!

Buying and selling foreclosure properties is not a get-rich-quick scheme. It's also not easy: It takes time, dedication, and real effort on your part to succeed. Don't put in the effort, and you won't succeed.

Successful real estate investors share some common traits. They treat investing as a business, objectively analyzing each deal for its risk and reward. They can communicate effectively. (We're not talking "slick" here. You don't have to be a polished public speaker, but you do have to be able to express yourself clearly so others understand your requirements, your goals, and your intentions.) They seek win-win situations with homeowners and build long-term business relationships with lenders, contractors, real estate agents, and other professionals. And finally, they demonstrate a real commitment to success: They're willing to work hard, to overcome problems, and to stick to their plans and their goals even when times are tough.

Experience is helpful, but effort and dedication are crucial. No amount of knowledge will help you if you're not willing to put in the time and effort required to succeed. But this is true of anything that is worthwhile and profitable.

 Almost every real estate investor has lost money on one or more transactions, even big-name investors like "The Donald." What makes these investors successful is that they learn from their mistakes and the mistakes of others, and manage to string together more successes than failures. To minimize your risk, start with one property and build in enough buffer (20% or more) so you won't lose your shirt. Eventually, as you gain experience, you can take on more properties.

MYTH # **9**

Real Estate Agents Won't Help Me with Foreclosures—There's Nothing in It for Them.

Fact: A Real Estate Agent Can Give You a Second Opinion Before You Buy and Then List the Property for You When You Sell

Real estate agents make no money when you buy a foreclosure property, but that doesn't mean smart agents still won't help you!

Why? Because real estate agents do not earn salaries; they earn commissions—typically 6 to 7% of the sale price. Agents earn commissions in two ways:

1. The agent finds a buyer for a listed property (*listed* means the property is being marketed by a real estate agency).
2. The agent lists a property that is eventually purchased, either by a purchaser he or she finds or by a purchaser found by another agent. If another agent finds the buyer, the listing agent (seller's agent) and the buyer's agent split the commission: Typically, the listing brokerage receives 50% and the selling brokerage receives 50%. If the listing agent also finds the buyer, the entire commission is earned

by the listing brokerage. The agent or broker then receives a portion of his or her brokerage's share of the commission.

When you're considering a property, an agent can also provide you with *comps*. Comps (*comparables*) are the prices of recently sold homes similar to the property you're considering. Comps help you determine the current value of a property as well as give an indication of what a property could eventually sell for. Agents can also provide inside information about the neighborhood, the area, and past history of the property, as well as a feel for the overall real estate market.

So if an agent won't make money by helping you evaluate a foreclosure property, why should they help?

If you plan to flip the property, the agent can list it and earn a commission on the sale. (Agents love to list properties, because they make money when the property sells even if they didn't find the buyer.) And real estate agents love to work with investors because investors are a source of repeat business. A smart real estate agent will be happy to provide advice and guidance on properties you're thinking of purchasing in return for the opportunity to list the properties you flip.

How can you find a good agent? First get recommendations from friends and family. If those leads don't prove to be worthwhile, an easy way to evaluate agents is by visiting open houses. Every weekend, agents across America hold open houses, inviting the public in to view properties for sale. Besides gaining the opportunity to meet real estate agents, you can learn a lot about what makes a house more attractive to potential buyers, and you can pick up tips to help you fix up properties for quick resale.

You can also evaluate the agent in action. Here are qualities to look for:

- ◆ Does the agent immediately greet you?
- ◆ Is she polite and helpful?
- ◆ Does she offer to show you around the house?
- ◆ Does she try to get to know you and find out what you're looking for?

You should be instantly impressed by a good real estate agent's enthusiasm and people skills. After all, those are qualities you want in an agent who's working for you. If you're impressed so far, ask the agent a few questions:

- ◆ What are her qualifications and experience?
- ◆ How long has she been selling real estate, especially in this area?
- ◆ How many houses has she sold in the last three to six months? What is the dollar value of the properties she sold last year?
- ◆ Does she or has she ever worked on foreclosure or *real-estate-owned* (REO) properties? Explain that you plan to invest in real estate, in particular in foreclosure properties. Also explain you are looking for an agent to help you evaluate and assess potential purchases, and in exchange you will offer her the opportunity to list the properties you purchase. Then ask how she feels about that kind of working relationship.

Interview two or three agents who impress you. Then, to make your choice, follow these guidelines:

- ◆ Choose an agent with at least two years in the business.
- ◆ Evaluate the answers you received. Does the agent seem knowledgeable? Does the agent inspire confidence? Trust your instincts in these regards.
- ◆ Most importantly, choose the agent you feel you'll be most comfortable working with. Remember you're hoping to establish a long-term working relationship; make sure it's a relationship you can both profit from and enjoy.

Good agents know their markets, and they're willing to share their knowledge. Smart agents will be willing to help you on the front end of a purchase for the opportunity to profit with you on the back end of the purchase when you sell.

Some agents also list REO (real-estate-owned) properties for banks. These are properties that the bank foreclosed on and then had to take possession of because no investor bid on the property at auction. The agent may not be able to offer you a great deal on REO properties, because he is supposed to get the highest price possible for the bank, but if the agent knows that you have the cash to close quickly and that's what the bank wants, you may be able to negotiate an attractive purchase price.

MYTH # **10**

I Can Do This by Myself.

Fact: Of Course You Can, but Why Should You?

Building a team dramatically increases your chances for success, and with the right team in place you can handle more opportunities each year and generate enough additional revenue to more than cover the expense of having more people on board.

How many people do you know who succeed on their own? We're guessing not many. In Myth #8, we explained why you don't have to be an expert, and that's especially true if you have help on your side. Let's look at how you can build a top-notch team of real estate professionals, including an agent, lender, attorney, home inspector, title company, and contractor. Each of these professionals makes a living providing services to people like you—and they'll want to be on your team:

Real Estate Agent. An agent will help you sell the properties you buy and provide you with comps for properties you're considering and inside information about the neighborhood, the area, and the real estate market. Experienced agents can also recommend other possible candidates for your team. We discussed how to find a good agent in Myth #9.

Mortgage Broker. Mortgage brokers help you secure financing. A good mortgage broker/loan officer has the following qualifications:

- ◆ Is state licensed.
- ◆ Is a member of the National Association of Mortgage Brokers (NAMB), the Mortgage Brokers Association (MBA), or both.
- ◆ Has at least five years experience, and has earned professional designations.

- Understands the foreclosure process and can help you borrow on the future value of the property, not just based on the purchase price. The future value is the *repaired value* of a property that is in disrepair; by sourcing funds based on the future value, you'll have access to more capital to finance repairs and renovations.
- Has earned positive references from past clients as well as from industry professionals, including real estate agents and title companies.

Attorney. Attorneys are specialists, and some specialize in real estate transactions. Ask your real estate agent for recommendations or call the local Board of Realtors and ask for the name and phone number of the attorney who represents them. Look for an attorney who is responsive, who returns your calls promptly, and who seems interested in working with you. Foreclosures often happen quickly, and your attorney must be able to respond quickly as well.

Home Inspector. A licensed home inspector evaluates the quality and condition of a home. If you purchase a property at a foreclosure auction, you often agree to purchase the property *as is* without having the chance to make an inspection. If you intend to purchase a property in foreclosure before the auction (*pre-foreclosure*), you can conduct the inspection beforehand or make the sale conditional on the home passing inspection.

Some localities have city inspectors available. City inspectors tend to be more up to date on local building codes and zoning changes. Your local government office can tell you whether city inspectors are available. In some areas, city inspectors are used exclusively for new construction.

Here are some of the items home inspectors evaluate:

- Structure
- Exterior
- Roofing
- Windows
- Siding
- Plumbing
- Electrical

- Heating
- Air conditioning
- Fireplaces

Home inspectors check the condition of each item and provide a report summarizing their findings.

To find a good home inspector, ask your title company, real estate agent, and other members of your team for referrals. Another excellent way to find licensed professional home inspectors in your area is through the American Society of Home Inspectors. Visit their web site at www.ASHI.com, and enter your ZIP code in the "Find a Home Inspector" box.

Tip: A retired contractor who is now working as a home inspector is often the best choice. Such a person not only can point out problems but also can give you a rough estimate of how much it will cost to fix.

Title Company. A title is a legal document that grants ownership of a piece of property to someone. A title company serves two main purposes:

- Conducts research to review the property's history and ensure there are no existing problems on the property title.
- Provides title insurance to insure legal conveyance of the property title.

The title company takes care of the paperwork and legalities of completing a title transfer. The title company you choose should understand the foreclosure process, because then they will know the common problems to look for in the title history—and how to clear them.

Contractors. A general contractor is an individual or a company hired to work on construction of a property. The general contractor typically employs or hires subcontractors who specialize in areas like plumbing, electrical work, and so forth. When you buy a property, it may need repair or renovation. You might need someone to install new plumbing, electrical wiring, flooring, or windows, or to repair the roof. A contractor can handle these tasks for you.

Unless the repairs or renovations needed are extensive, you can serve as the general contractor, hiring subcontractors to help you. But if you're unsure about your skills or the time you'll have available, considering hiring a general contractor. Time is money.

Get recommendations from your real estate agent and other real estate investors to find honest and reliable contractors.

While we're talking about building a team, let's talk about partners. A good partner can help you achieve more than you could ever achieve on your own. (Of course, a bad partner can make your life a nightmare!)

If you decide to create a partnership, pick someone whose talents and skills complement yours. For example, if you aren't comfortable directing contractors, consider bringing in a partner to oversee property repairs and renovations. You may be great at evaluating properties and arranging financing, and your partner may excel at managing repairs and renovations.

If you do create a partnership, have your attorney draft a contract detailing your responsibilities and your business arrangement. Don't work on a handshake basis—if things go badly, your partnership agreement will help minimize the damage.

 If you do partner up with someone, make sure you both have control of the money. You should both be required to sign any checks to pay for repairs and renovations. Neither party should blindly trust the other when it comes to matters of money. You should both be in the know and share decisions on how that money is spent.

SECTION 2

The Foreclosure Process

The foreclosure process itself can take anywhere from 30 days to over a year to play out, depending on the rules and regulations that govern foreclosure in your area (see the Appendix for your state's requirements). As an investor, you can purchase properties at any stage of the process—directly from homeowners in pre-foreclosure, at the foreclosure auction or sale, or from another investor or the bank after the foreclosure sale. In addition, the distressed homeowners have certain rights at each stage of the process that may provide you with additional options.

To successfully and safely invest in foreclosures, it pays to know how the foreclosure process is carried out in your area and the approximate time limits for each stage of the process. This enables you to provide accurate information to any homeowners you happen to deal with, lets you know what you can expect at each stage, and empowers you to protect your own rights as an investor.

Unfortunately, many myths and misconceptions surround the foreclosure process and may give you a false impression of what actually takes place. In this section, we bust through the most common myths.

MYTH # **11**

The Process Takes a Long Time.

Fact: The Maximum Amount of Time Required to Foreclose Varies

The time required to foreclose on a home—from the time the homeowner stops making payments until the bank or an investor takes possession of the home—can vary greatly depending on the rules and regulations that govern foreclosure in a particular area and on how the foreclosure process happens to unfold. In areas that allow judicial foreclosures, for example, the homeowner may be able to drag out the process indefinitely by filing one motion after another.

In some states, where the process is not handled through the courts and where the homeowners have no redemption period, the process can be wrapped up in 30 days. Some take longer. In our home state of Michigan, for example, most homeowners have six months after the auction to redeem their property by buying it back from the bank or the investor who purchased it at the auction; some homeowners have as long as 12 months.

Note: The redemption period is the time after the sale (auction) when the homeowners have the right, but not the obligation, to buy back their property. In order to redeem their home, the homeowners have to pay off the balance of their loan or the price the buyer paid at auction (whichever is greater) plus all taxes, penalties, interest, and other qualifying expenses the buyer of the home paid and filed an affidavit for having paid. In extreme cases, the redemption period can be up to one year. To determine your state's redemption period, contact your local county or city offices, or check in the Appendix at the back of the book.

What's important is that you know how much time a typical foreclosure requires and the maximum amount of time it takes. If you buy a home planning to sell it in 30 days when the homeowner has 90 days to live there rent-free, you may be sorely disappointed to find out that the law is not on your side, especially if you have to pay property taxes and insurance for those 90 days, and the people living in "your home" are not paying you rent.

Tip: In areas that have a lengthy redemption period, you may be able to convince the homeowners to move out sooner by offering them cash for handing over the keys and for signing an agreement to move out. Just make sure they're on their way out before you hand over the money!

Even if you do purchase foreclosures in an area where the foreclosure process is lengthy, you don't have to take on the time-consuming and often complicated repairs and renovations in order to make money on foreclosures. Instead, you can serve as the *bird dog*—finding and buying foreclosures and then quickly turning around and selling them to other investors for a modest profit. This practice needs to be handled responsibly, though, as this could be seen as taking advantage of distressed homeowners— something we don't advocate!

Some investors are eager to buy investment properties but don't know how to find them—or aren't willing to do the work necessary to find them. Many are part-time investors who hold full-time jobs. They have cash to invest and the resources to rehab a property, but they don't have the time to find, analyze, and act on deals. When you provide them with good deals, you and the investor win.

What is the main advantage of this approach? You don't spend time and money (money that you may not even have) performing any repairs. You simply make money from finding a great deal for another investor. The disadvantage is that you won't make as much money on each deal, and you could even find yourself buying a house that you can't line up an investor to purchase from you.

Working with another investor can take two basic forms. The investor could put up all the money, including the cashier's check you'll need at the foreclosure auction. You'll purchase the property in his or her name and receive a fee for your efforts. Or, you could purchase the property at auction using your funds and then assign the contract to the investor. (*Assigning* a contract means another party "buys" the contract from you for a fee; once the contract is assigned, the new owner of the contract enjoys all the rights conferred by that contract. The other party—the seller of the property—is still bound by the provisions of the contract.)

Unless you have another investor or partner lined up, don't automatically assume you can flip a contract in a month or less. Obstacles and roadblocks do pop up; make sure you can afford to hold the property for several months, just in case. If you can't afford that, don't make the purchase unless you're sure your ducks are in a row.

Some disreputable investors in areas that offer homeowners a redemption period attempt to speed up the process by deceiving homeowners. They purchase the property at auction and show up at the home the next day telling the owners that they must vacate the premises immediately, even though the owners have the legal right to stay longer. We strongly discourage such practices. Disreputable investors don't last, and if there's any justice in the world, they do jail time.

MYTH # **12**

I Can't Get It—It's in Bankruptcy.

Fact: Properties in Bankruptcy Proceedings Must Be Sold to Satisfy Creditors

First a quick caveat: Investing in bankruptcies is not for the faint of heart. Instead of dealing with distressed homeowners or bidding at an auction, you'll be dealing with attorneys or court-appointed trustees, both of whom are committed to getting market value—or failing that, the highest price possible—for the property. Creditors can also oppose the sale of the property. What seems simple can become a tangled and complicated web. If you're new to real estate investing, wait until you have some experience under your belt —and an attorney who specializes in bankruptcies in your corner.

With that said, you can find great opportunities buying properties in bankruptcy, if for no other reason than many investors steer clear due to the effort involved.

Here's the bottom line. A property in a bankruptcy must be sold to satisfy creditors. Creditors don't want the house; they want their money back. The bankruptcy trustee's goal is to maximize the money generated to satisfy as many creditors as possible in a relatively short period of time. To navigate the bankruptcy waters, you'll need to work hard to get the trustees, the attorneys, and sometimes even the homeowners to look favorably upon you and your offer—and you'll need to make sure everything you do is reviewed and approved by a skilled attorney who will look out for your interests. (We'll look more closely at buying bankruptcy properties in Myth #34.)

Although not recommended for the beginner, you *can* purchase properties in bankruptcy—but you absolutely must know what you are doing.

 Pick an area you want to specialize in and stick with it. If you're going to invest in pre-foreclosures, focus all of your efforts on dealing with homeowners early in the process. If you're going to purchase properties in bankruptcy, start networking with bankruptcy attorneys. You can expand into other areas of foreclosure later.

MYTH # **13**

I Can't Help Out the Homeowner.

Fact: In Pre-Foreclosure You Can Offer Homeowners Numerous Options, All of Which Are Better than the Option Most People Take—Doing Nothing

Imagine you're a homeowner facing foreclosure. You don't know where to turn for help or guidance, and you have no idea where you could possibly find the money to dig yourself out of your financial hole. Your credit is already damaged, you may lose any equity you have in the home, and if you're foreclosed on, your credit will be damaged even further. The picture is bleak: Experts estimate that approximately 90% of homeowners are so far in debt and so underinformed that they mistakenly believe they have only two options—pay up or move out.

How can you help? As someone who knows the foreclosure process and has access to cash, you can assist these distressed homeowners in any number of ways:

- Present them with reliable information and options they may not have considered.
- Inform them of their rights as a homeowner.
- Encourage them to take action before they run out of time and options.
- Encourage them to borrow from friends or relatives to reinstate the mortgage, so they have more time to sell the home or to regain their financial footing.
- Negotiate a short sale with the lender on behalf of the homeowners, so they can sell the home without losing money. (With a short sale, the lender agrees to accept as payment in full a partial payment of the total balance owed.)
- Buy the home from them in pre-foreclosure, so they can maintain their dignity and what's left of their credit rating and perhaps cash out some of their equity. We estimate that selling an unaffordable home is the best option for about 90% of homeowners facing foreclosure. (Just make sure that the purchase price you pay is low enough for you to earn a fair profit.)
- Enable them to receive more of the equity they have built up in the home. If they lose the home in foreclosure, they stand to lose all the equity they have in the home, too. If you buy it prior to the auction, you may be able to get yourself a good deal while sharing some of the equity with the homeowners.
- Buy the home in foreclosure (to wipe out any junior liens against the home) and then sell it back to the homeowners on contract or lease it back to them until they are in a better position to move. (Be careful with this option. The liens may reattach to the home if you

sell it back to the homeowners, or the homeowners may not be able to make the payments you require.)

You may notice that a couple of these options, such as convincing the homeowners to borrow money from relatives to reinstate the mortgage, could result in a lost opportunity for you to take possession of the home. In order to act with integrity, you must accept the fact that you may not get the house all the time. To retain a positive reputation and keep yourself out of legal trouble, do the right thing. Ideally, you want to create win-win situations or at least situations in which you win and the homeowner doesn't lose too much—situations in which the homeowner can move forward and leave a bad experience in his past.

Purchasing a home directly from the homeowners in pre-foreclosure provides the homeowners another benefit. You can give them a little more control over when they will need to vacate the premises. Depending on the circumstances, you could even agree to purchase the home and lease it back to the original owners, allowing them to remain in the home (even though they no longer own it). This is often an attractive option for families with children who will soon graduate from school; they can remain in the home until their kids graduate, so they don't have to change schools and break off relationships with childhood friends.

Buying at pre-foreclosure also offers advantages to you. You'll have a chance to inspect the house thoroughly, so you'll know exactly what repairs may be necessary. You'll have more time to arrange financing, and you'll face less competition from other investors since the foreclosure won't be announced to the public. And, if your area gives foreclosed-upon homeowners the opportunity for redemption, you'll avoid that process.

STOP Helping a homeowner in distress should never involve taking advantage of the person. You should never misrepresent yourself as an attorney or financial professional if you're not. Act with integrity and professionalism at all times. Homeowners in financial distress face bleak prospects; never take advantage of their misfortune. If you can develop a win-win pre-foreclosure option, great! Short-term profits never outweigh damage to your reputation or honor.

MYTH # **14**

They'll Save the Property, and I'll Be Out My Time and Money.

Fact: Occasionally You May Be Out Your Time, But Most Properties Aren't Saved from Foreclosure; Plus, You'll Gain Valuable Experience from Each Deal You Investigate, Even if You Don't End Up with the Home

Some properties that enter the foreclosure process are not foreclosed upon. Homeowners may bring their payments current by selling other assets, getting help from families, or through other means. (But as we noted in the previous Myth, only about 10% of these homeowners are able to avoid foreclosure.)

Still others may get their homes back through redemption. The odds are slim, however, since redemption requires that the balance of the loan be paid off plus all accumulated interest, penalties, and taxes. Homeowners who can't make their monthly payments are very unlikely to suddenly find the funds necessary to pay off the loan in full.

But let's say you have worked hard to evaluate a foreclosure purchase: You and your team have analyzed the deal, developed comps, estimated potential repair costs, and arranged financing. You've put your usual effort into doing your homework, and the homeowners manage to save the property. You're out some amount of time—and time is money—but you'll also have gained additional experience. Every property you evaluate is like another notch in your belt, because you'll develop a stronger rapport with your team and you'll learn lessons you can apply down the road. You can learn something new from every situation: Even deals that don't go through provide valuable, real-world training you'll never get in a classroom.

If a homeowner does save a property, good for him! You may have missed an investment opportunity, but he was able to keep his *home*. It's hard to be too disappointed if you think of it that way.

If you've been working with homeowners in pre-foreclosure who ultimately save their home, send them a card or letter congratulating them. If they end up in trouble later and need to sell their home, they will be more likely to remember your kindness and consider selling to you rather than some less compassionate investor. In addition, if they have friends or family members facing foreclosure, they will think of referring them to you.

MYTH # **15**

They Can Still Cancel the Sale.

Fact: The Homeowners Do Not Have the Ability to Cancel the Sale

Once the foreclosure process is underway, the *lender* can cancel the sale, but only if the homeowner brings payments current (which as you know is unlikely), they sell the home in pre-foreclosure (possibly to you!), or they file for bankruptcy.

Keep in mind that the lender does not wish to foreclose. Lenders are in the business of lending money, not selling real estate. Banks aren't permitted to make a profit on real estate sales; in fact, banks operate under federal regulations prohibiting them from being in the business of selling real estate at all. Instead, banks want a predictable stream of revenue and do not want the hassle and headaches involved in taking over a property and selling it. But if they have no other recourse, they will foreclose.

There are only a few ways the sale can be canceled: The homeowner brings the account current, the home is purchased in pre-foreclosure (either case rendering an auction unnecessary), or the homeowners declare bankruptcy and the property is then tied up in bankruptcy proceedings. (As soon as the homeowners file for bankruptcy, the court issues a *stay*, which basically freezes everything, prohibiting collectors from proceeding with their attempts to collect on money owed them. Creditors can file to have the stay lifted. If the court lifts the stay, then any lenders who have liens against the property can move forward with foreclosure proceedings.)

Aside from bringing payments current, the only way the homeowner can cancel the sale is by declaring bankruptcy, but most choose not to. Foreclosure is a bad situation for a homeowner; bankruptcy has even more significant ramifications. In foreclosure, the house is lost; in bankruptcy, other assets besides the house may be lost as well. For some homeowners, however, particularly those who are buried in unsecured debt, such as credit card debt, bankruptcy could be the best option.

If homeowners are running out of time, you may be able to lend them the money to reinstate their mortgage and buy yourself some additional time to purchase the home from them. When lending money to homeowners, you need to be careful, however, and have contracts in place to make sure the homeowners can't claim that they thought it was a gift or some other gesture of goodwill. We strongly encourage you to consult an attorney experienced in foreclosures for guidance in legal matters and to draw up any contracts between you and the homeowners.

MYTH # **16**

I Have to Wait Until It's Listed with a Real Estate Agent.

Fact: Foreclosures Aren't Sold by Agents

Waiting for an agent to list a foreclosure property guarantees a long—okay, endless—wait. Foreclosure properties simply are not listed by agents. The only time agents may get involved is if the homeowners hire an agent to list their home in pre-foreclosure or the bank hires an agent to list an REO property that it acquired at a foreclosure sale.

Remember the stages of foreclosure: The homeowner gets behind on payments, the lender takes steps to try to remedy the situation, the attorney gets involved, and eventually the house is sold at auction. Real estate agents may get involved in pre- or post-foreclosure, but they rarely show up during the actual foreclosure process.

A homeowner in distress can certainly sell her home, because the owner can sell the home at any time she chooses. And she can decide to list her home with an agent to facilitate the sale. A homeowner in the foreclosure process can also attempt to sell her home, with or without the help of an agent, because she is still the lawful owner of the property.

But, if the homeowner is unable to sell the home before the auction occurs, she loses the right to sell the home because the sale transfers ownership to the winner of the auction, or, if there is no winning bidder, to the lender. If the lender takes possession, the property becomes a *real-estate-owned* (REO) property, and at that point the lender will likely list the property with an agent. (We'll cover REO properties thoroughly in Myth #21.)

To find foreclosure properties for sale, check your newspaper or check the records at your courthouse.

Some investors do quite well buying REO properties, but the ones who really excel in this area are investors who work closely with banks and obtain leads on REO properties before the properties are listed through an agent. Once the agent lists the home, he wants to get top dollar for it, because his commission is a percentage of the sale price.

MYTH # **17**

It Was Published in the Paper, So I Can Buy It Now.

Fact: Publishing Simply Notifies the Public the Foreclosure Process Is Underway

Again, remember the stages of foreclosure. The foreclosure notice or Notice of Default is an official announcement to the public that the foreclosure process has begun for a particular property. The property can't be bought until the foreclosure auction, except in pre-foreclosure, which we'll cover in the next Myth.

— 33 —

While it may seem harsh and unforgiving, the foreclosure process is actually designed to protect homeowners and give them a fair and reasonable opportunity to keep their home. The process ensures the homeowner has time to secure additional funds, seek help from friends and family, work with the lender to make acceptable repayment arrangements, or even sell the home to satisfy the debt. And in states with lengthy redemption periods (Kentucky, for example, has a redemption period of 12 months), the homeowners still have a chance to regain ownership of the home if they can gather the funds to pay off the loan balance and all interest, penalties, and taxes.

As a result, every property that enters foreclosure will not necessarily be sold, either in pre-foreclosure or at auction. But statistically speaking, the majority will be, once all stages of the foreclosure process have taken place. The Notice of Default or foreclosure notice is your signal to check out the opportunity and start evaluating the possibilities.

 Foreclosure notices usually must be published for several consecutive weeks. When you spot a foreclosure notice for a property that catches your eye, cut out the notice and add it to a file you created for the home. Sometimes, a foreclosure notice will appear once or twice and then fail to show up in the third or fourth week, meaning something interrupted the proceedings. By following the notices, you can get a better feel for the progression.

MYTH # **18**

I Have to Wait Until the Auction to Buy the Property.

Fact: Not if You Buy from the Owner

The time period between the foreclosure notice and the foreclosure auction is known as *pre-foreclosure*. Pre-foreclosure purchases are in many ways similar to a normal real estate purchase: You negotiate with the homeowner, sign a contract (purchase agreement), and proceed with the transaction. The main difference is that instead of the homeowner deciding on his own to sell the property, you'll contact the homeowner in order to try to buy his house when he's facing financial difficulties and the likelihood of foreclosure.

As we've already mentioned, you can easily find homeowners in the early stages of foreclosure by checking public notices. The public notice will list the lender's attorney, and you can contact the lawyer for additional information about the property. Don't be surprised if she's friendly but not particularly cooperative: The lawyer provides legal services, and acting as a receiver for the property is only one of those services. The lawyer is paid to prepare paperwork and conduct the foreclosure sale, not to act as a real estate information hotline.

If you're interested in the property, you'll eventually need to contact the homeowner directly. Keep in mind that the homeowner is already under a considerable amount of pressure and is not likely, at least at first, to respond positively to your approach. You'll need to be tactful, respectful, and aware at all times that the homeowner is under a great deal of stress and strain.

Why? Even if it's in their best interest, most homeowners don't want to give up their homes. They will desperately hold onto the hope that things will somehow work out. Most are also upset they're facing foreclosure, even if they find themselves in that position through their own mistakes or poor choices.

If the homeowner is receptive to your approach, the first thing you'll need to determine is whether there is equity in the home. Let's say, for example, that the home has a fair market value of $200,000. You've been able to inspect the home, and other than cosmetic repairs, it's in great shape. You estimate you'll spend $10,000 getting the house ready to sell. So, you decide your walk-away price is $160,000, which leaves you room to make the profit you want while covering repair and holding costs.

If the homeowner still owes $180,000 on the mortgage, you're not likely to buy it for $160,000. (Although occasionally a homeowner may take less than the amount he owes, the chances are slim.) And if a judgment has been entered, the homeowner most likely will have to come up with the total amount of money required to satisfy the judgment, which at the very least will require the loan be paid off in full. The homeowner needs to realize the whole loan amount from the sale in order to pay off the loan.

If the homeowner has limited equity in the property, you're unlikely to be able to negotiate a price dramatically lower than the home's value. And if you can't buy below market value, you'll never make a profit.

(If you can negotiate a short sale with the lender on the homeowner's behalf, however, you may be able to purchase the home for less than the current balance owed on it without the homeowner's having to make up the difference, as discussed later in this Myth.)

Buying at pre-foreclosure does have several advantages. The homeowner may be desperate and willing to do almost anything to avoid actual foreclosure. (In many cases, his options are limited, however.) In addition, you can enter the property to inspect it before purchasing, unlike when you purchase at auction. And, if you contact the homeowner directly and the homeowner has not listed the property, the homeowner will avoid paying a commission to an agent, which could allow you to benefit from those savings in the form of a lower purchase price. (The average real estate commission is 6%, which would come to $12,000 on a $200,000 sales price.)

Buying pre-foreclosure properties can be a win-win situation for you and the homeowner: You may be able to find great deals, and the homeowner can escape a very ugly financial situation. But before you contact a homeowner, keep these things in mind:

- Never mislead the homeowner. Never represent yourself as a lawyer, an accountant, financial advisor, or real estate agent (unless you actually are, of course). Unless you truly plan to live in the home, state up front that you're an investor.
- Don't make friends with the homeowner solely to convince him to sell the property to you.
- Recommend that the homeowner contact his lender and his attorney to get advice. Don't try to circumvent other interested parties.
- Put all agreements and offers in writing. In real estate transactions, verbal agreements don't stand up in court.

Let the homeowners decide what is best for them. Don't simply look out for your best interests. Your goal is a win-win result: Discuss the other options they have, including bankruptcy. Don't try to influence: In this and in all matters, represent yourself professionally and with integrity.

Sometimes, negotiating a win-win-win situation with the homeowner, the lender, and yourself may seem impossible. In the example we presented in this Myth, where the homeowner owes $180,000 on a home that's worth about $200,000 and requires $10,000 in repairs, you might think that you can't possibly work out a solution. However, you may be able to negotiate a *short sale* with the lender, in which the lender agrees to accept $160,000 as full payment. Now, the deal looks much more attractive, and the homeowner doesn't have to sell at a loss.

MYTH # **19**

If I'm Not the High Bidder at Auction, I Can Forget Buying the House.

Fact: As with Any Transaction, Pitfalls Can Still Derail the Sale

Have you ever sold a car—or thought you had an agreement to sell a car—only to have the sale fall apart later? The same thing happens every day in real estate transactions, and it also happens with foreclosure auction purchases. For example, the high bidder may not arrange financing in time.

To get a sense of what can keep the high bidder from purchasing the property, first let's look more closely at the bidding process. This is a great time to give you the insider's view of a foreclosure auction.

Foreclosure auctions are held in publicly accessible locations. The old stereotype of an auction on the courthouse steps is often true: If the notice refers to the sale being held on the courthouse steps, it literally means the steps outside the courthouse.

Last-minute postponements are relatively common. The action could be resolved or postponed at the last minute for a variety of reasons, such as the homeowners reinstating the loan, filing for bankruptcy, or filing a complaint with the court that the lender failed to properly notify them. You can always call the attorney in charge of the sale or the Register of Deeds office the day before to make sure the sale is still on.

You probably won't be alone on the steps. If you're interested in the property, expect others to show interest as well. Sometimes, nobody shows up!

Rules and regulations vary according to locality, but in most cases you'll need to have cash or a cashier's check for at least 10% of the purchase price of the property or $10,000, whichever is higher. You'll also be required to arrange financing and complete the purchase of the property within a short period of time—the term varies according to your locality. If you don't manage to arrange financing, you can lose your deposit, but if you petition the auctioneer you can sometimes get your deposit returned. There is no guarantee that will happen, though, so you should bid only if you're sure you have adequate financing prearranged.

The sale then begins with a recital of the action by what most localities call the *referee*. The referee is the receiver, and has the power to execute the sale even without the homeowner's signature. (Remember the covenants.) After the introduction is concluded, the sale begins.

The opening bid is usually made by the lender. This bid is often called the "upset price." The upset price is the amount due the lender, including the mortgage balance, late payment charges, and all costs incurred in initiating and handling the foreclosure. The upset price gives you an indication of what the lender needs to get from the property in order to avoid losing money.

Lenders are under no obligation to identify themselves, and occasionally they won't bid at all. While it may not make sense that someone owed money secured by a property will refuse to bid on that property, it does happen. If the lender doesn't bid, there's usually a good reason—and that should raise a red flag.

Remember, as the creditor, the lender carries no responsibility for maintenance, repair, upkeep, or other costs. If the lender knows of major problems with the property, it may not bid. As long as the lender doesn't actually own the property, the lender's just another interested party. Once the lender owns the property—which it will if it bids and no one else does—then it assumes all the responsibilities and the costs of ownership.

Here's the bottom line: If the lender doesn't bid, then you probably don't want the property unless you have inside knowledge. (For example, you may have been able to inspect the property and determine that what appeared at first glance to be a major foundation problem is actually a minor cosmetic issue.) The problem is, as you've probably guessed, you may not know whether the lender has bid unless you're familiar with all the parties involved in the auction. That's why attending a number of auctions as an observer will help give you a sense of who the major players normally are, and how to identify a lender's representative even if she does not announce herself as such.

Lenders can make a claim only for the amount of the judgment and no more. If the winning bid is for a greater amount than the judgment, the remaining funds, or surplus monies, go to junior lien holders, and if any money is left, the homeowner has the right to claim the remainder. Very seldom will there be surplus monies; auction bidders are looking for great deals and almost always want to pay significantly less than market price for the property.

Frequently the amount of the judgment is higher than what investors are willing to pay. If the lender is the high bidder, as often happens, the bank is now the owner of the property and the lender is required to sell the property. (We'll look at purchasing bank- or lender-owned properties, or REO properties, a little later.)

So what can go wrong? The high bidder—not the lender—may not be able to arrange financing, and the sale doesn't go through. Or the lender may be the high bidder, in which case there really hasn't been a sale; ownership has simply been transferred to the lender until the lender can sell the property. Properties "sold" at foreclosure auction often can be available for purchase days later.

STOP Never bid on a house unless you have a certified check for an amount sufficient to cover the down payment and can come up with the rest of the cash by the required deadline. The people who hold the auction have very little patience with novice investors who place bids and then fail to follow through with the purchase. In some areas, you may be required to show your certified check before being allowed to place a bid. And if you bid and then fail to follow through with the purchase, you may be banned from bidding in future auctions.

Finding the "Right" Properties

Real estate investors live by the credo, "You make your profit when you buy." This means that if you buy the right property for the right price, you are almost assured that your investment will be a profitable one. Buy the wrong property for too much money, and no matter what you do from that point on, you are almost destined to lose money.

In foreclosure investing as in most potentially profitable ventures, knowledge is power. People who buy stuff at garage sales and sell it on eBay for 100 to 1,000% more than they paid for it make money because they know what they can sell the "junk" for on eBay. People who buy and sell antiques for a profit know more than the people they are buying from about how much they can sell the items for on the open market. In the same way, you can profit from foreclosures only if you know how much a property is worth and have a pretty good idea of what it will cost to fix it up and sell it.

Finding the "right" property can make or break a deal and mean thousands to you in profits or losses. Here we tackle the common myths about how to narrow down your search to only the properties that have the greatest profit potential and save loads of time in the process.

MYTH # **20**

Every Foreclosure Is a Good Deal.

Fact: You Need to Know the Market Value of What You're Buying

Perhaps the biggest myth in the world of foreclosures is that just because a property is foreclosed on it's a great deal. That's like believing everything you find at The Dollar Store is cheaper than you can get it at the grocery store or Wal-Mart. The fact is that you need to shop for foreclosures and do your research so that you have a pretty good idea of what you're getting yourself into, what exactly it is you're buying, how much it will probably cost to fix up and sell, and how much of a profit you can reasonably expect.

Novice investors usually get burned when they fail to perform their due diligence. Before you even think about presenting a purchase agreement to homeowners in pre-foreclosure or placing a bid at an auction, you should research the following carefully:

- **Title:** Order a title commitment from a reputable, local title company, which will show the chain of title along with the current homeowners' names, all liens against the property (including first and second mortgages), property taxes paid or due, and delinquent water bills or other services supplied by the municipality. You can also pick up a copy of the title at the Register of Deeds office, typically located in the county courthouse.
- **Foreclosure notice:** The foreclosure notice contains all sorts of useful information, including the case or reference number; county in which the property is located; legal lot, legal description, parcel ID #, subdivision, and city (which you can use to obtain the mailing address for the property); name of the mortgagors (the borrowers); name of the mortgagee (lender); amount owed on the mortgage; interest rate of the loan; lender's attorney; sale date; length of property's redemption period (if any); and Liber (the legal book in which the deed is recorded at the county courthouse) and page number of the mortgage.

- **Mortgage and note:** These documents are recorded with the Register of Deeds. It's a good idea to get a copy of the mortgage and promissory note, so you can check out what the homeowners agreed to in the contracts they signed promising repayment of the debt to the lender.
- **Property worksheet:** Every town, city, or county in the United States keeps a worksheet on every property, showing when it was built, any building permits issued, any code violations, inspection reports, and so on. This gives you some idea of whether the home has a checkered past. Check with county or city building department.
- **Visual inspection of the home:** At the very least, you should visit the property and the neighborhood in which it is located and take a good look around. Inspect the outside of the property from all four sides, being careful not to trespass. Take photos, if possible. If you can get inside to take a look around, take plenty of notes and estimate the cost of repairs and renovations needed to make the home marketable.
- **Market values of comparable homes:** Check out the prices of comparable homes in the same neighborhood that have sold in the last six to eight weeks along with the asking prices of comparable homes that are currently listed for sale. You need to know the approximate price you will sell the home for after repairs and renovations before deciding how much to offer.

Foreclosure investing is no different from any other type of investing. In real estate investing, unless you plan to rent the property, your profit comes from the difference between the purchase price and the sale price. The difference must be large enough to cover all your costs and still generate the profit you're looking for. It's that simple. Some properties are terrible deals because you can never recover your costs and make a profit. Others are great deals because you can buy significantly below market value, make needed improvements, and still sell for a handsome profit. The only way to determine the possibilities is to analyze each opportunity.

We've just stated a very simple formula: Sale Price − (Purchase Price + Costs) = Profit. Each of the three variables (Sale Price, Purchase

Price, and Costs) is made up of smaller components. Some, like the purchase price, you have direct control over because you will determine what
you're willing to pay. The price you'll eventually sell the property for (Sale
Price), on the other hand, must be estimated. You can check out comps
to *predict* the fair market value of the property, but in the end the true
value of any property is what someone is ready and able to pay at that point
in time.

As an investor, you must purchase the property at a low enough price
to afford the holding costs and the necessary improvements and still make
a profit. If you plan to upgrade the property, you must have a low enough
purchase price so it supports the planned improvements—and again still
leaves room for profit. If you have no chance of making a profit, you should
not purchase the property.

Costs are the next variable in the profit equation, which include
holding the property, making repairs and improvements, insurance
and taxes, mortgage payments, and costs of sale. Some costs are easier to calculate than others. Here's a breakdown of the major costs
involved:

- **Holding Costs:** Holding costs include loan interest, taxes, and utilities. How long you hold the property determines the total cost. Many
  investors assume they'll hold a property for at least four months, assuming two months to make repairs and two months to sell the property. Your real estate agent and contractor can help you estimate the
  time it should take to make repairs and sell the property. (Keep in
  mind that how quickly a property sells is often a function of price; if
  you list the home at somewhat below fair market value, you're more
  likely to sell quickly; list above market value and you may hold the
  property for a long, long time.)
- **Repairs and Improvements:** Cosmetic improvements are relatively inexpensive; major improvements can cost tens of thousands
  of dollars and take months to complete. Regardless of what you plan,
  you must estimate the cost to determine whether a deal makes sense.
  The cost of repairs and improvements represents a major portion of
  the project's overall expense. In some cases, the market will not

support the cost of the repairs and improvements and return a decent profit.

- **Costs of Sale:** At the closing of a real estate deal, certain costs of the transaction are apportioned to the buyer and seller. The real estate commission is typically the highest-cost item, averaging 6% of the sale price. Legal fees and other costs are also included.

Whatever is left is *profit*.

Don't forget to consider the value of your time and effort. Real estate investing also involves *your* time: finding deals, evaluating deals, completing the purchase, making improvements, working with your team—the entire process takes a lot of time. Your time has value, so when you're evaluating a deal, first determine whether you have the time to devote to the project, and then whether the return you expect is worth your time. If it's not, find another deal. It's that simple.

Don't let the 6% commission that an agent charges to list your investment property for sale scare you off from hiring an agent. Studies show that a skilled Realtor can sell a home in half the time it takes homeowners to sell it themselves, and the higher price at which they sell more than covers their commission. You are likely to save on holding costs and command a higher sales price at the same time. In addition, you have more time to find, buy, and sell your next property.

MYTH # **21**

I'm Buying a Home at the Foreclosure Auction.

Fact: You Are Buying a Lien at the Foreclosure Auction

When a lender forecloses on a property, the lender does not want to take the home. The lender wants the money the homeowner borrowed against the home. Instead of taking the home, fixing it up, and placing it on the market—all of which would be a major hassle—the bank tries to sell the lien it holds against the property at auction. This lien can be a property tax lien, a first mortgage, a second mortgage, a construction or mechanic's lien, or any other piece of paper the homeowner signed using the home as collateral for the loan.

Any lien holder can choose to foreclose and sell its stake in the property via a foreclosure auction, assuming the homeowner is delinquent in making payments. When you place a bid at a foreclosure auction, you are not bidding on the property. You are bidding only on the lien.

The reason this is so important is because the foreclosure process can wipe out liens against the property based on the hierarchy of liens. According to the hierarchy of liens, some liens take precedence over others. A property tax lien holds the most power, followed by a first mortgage, followed by a second mortgage, and so on. Usually the lien that was placed on the home first has more precedence than those put in place later.

Let's look at an example of how this works. Say a homeowner owns a $350,000 house. She owes $250,000 on a first mortgage, $50,000 on a second mortgage, and $20,000 on a home equity line of credit. You buy the home equity line of credit lien at auction for $15,000. I buy the first mortgage for $260,000, bidding $10,000 more than what was owed on it.

Out of the $260,000 I pay, the lender holding the first mortgage receives $250,000. The holder of the second mortgage receives $10,000 and loses out on the other $40,000. You don't get a dime, because nothing is left to cover your $15,000 investment.

This happens more often than you might think when novice investors bid on what they believe are properties but are actually just liens against those properties.

STOP Don't buy the second unless you're going to buy the first. We advise novice investors to not even think about buying anything but property tax liens or first mortgages until they have gained some experience and know what they're doing. However, in situations where buying the second mortgage is a part of a savvy strategy, make sure you buy the first mortgage, too.

MYTH # **22**

Courthouse Auctions Are the Only Source of Foreclosure Properties.

Fact: Different Stages of the Foreclosure Process Offer Different Opportunities to Purchase Properties

When most people consider investing in foreclosures, they envision bidding on properties at foreclosure auctions. They think the homeowner can't pay, so the lender takes the property and places it on the auction block. The fact is that the process is more drawn out than that and offers opportunities to buy properties at any of several stages from before the auction (pre-foreclosure) to well after the auction (post-foreclosure).

Some investors focus on purchasing at a specific stage in the process. For example, we know investors who purchase only pre-foreclosures; they realize opportunities exist at auction, but they prefer working directly with homeowners. Others do not like interacting with homeowners and choose to wait until the auction. Still others focus exclusively on REO properties, preferring to work directly with lenders or with the lender's real estate agent. For the most part, successful investors are willing to purchase at any stage in the process as long as the deal makes sense.

Since we've already looked closely at pre-foreclosure and foreclosure auctions, this is a good opportunity to give you a solid understanding of *real-estate-owned* (REO) properties.

Buying REO properties offers a number of advantages for investors. Buying during the pre-foreclosure phase can create win-win situations, but also requires dealing with homeowners who are under a great deal of stress and financial pressure. Lenders, on the other hand, are professional operations, keeping normal office hours and following reliable procedures. More importantly, the lenders are motivated to sell the property for business reasons, and also because they're under the pressure of federal guidelines to not be in the "business" of real estate.

Lenders are eager to turn any liability—in this case, the properties they own (and the unpaid debt those properties represent)—into assets by selling them and getting them off their books. Lenders want to hold mortgages and receive payments, not spend money on upkeep, taxes, and the cost of selling properties. As a result, lenders often will offer incredible deals on their REO properties. One of the biggest reasons they're able to do so is due to *private mortgage insurance* (PMI).

Lenders require homeowners to purchase PMI when they finance more than 80% of the value of the home. (Unless you made a large down payment or have built up significant equity, you're probably paying PMI on your home.) The homeowner pays the premium even though the insurance covers the lender's risk: PMI protects mortgage lenders against potential losses in the event of borrower default, and covers the lender from loss if the lender sells a property for less than the judgment value.

The end result is that the lender has little incentive to maximize the price it gets for the property, since ultimately the homeowner and PMI must make up the difference between the sale price and the judgment price. In most cases, while it may sound harsh, the lender simply wants to unload the property.

You can fully inspect REO properties, because in most cases the lender has already evicted the previous owner. The lender now owns the property, so the lender can show it at any time. Remember, the biggest unknown involved in buying a property at the foreclosure auction is the condition of the house, since you can't get inside to inspect the interior before the purchase. With REO properties, you can inspect the house. You can bring a contractor in to provide an estimate, and you can create a detailed and accurate estimate of the cost and time required to return the property to marketable condition. You can make a very educated assessment of the investment potential in each property.

So how do you find out about REO properties? There are two basic ways to locate REO properties: through the bank or through real estate agents.

Many lenders have what they call *salvage* departments responsible for their inventory of REO properties. Some lenders even have property-management departments responsible for the maintenance, upkeep, and disposal of their REO inventory.

To find properties through lenders, simply call and ask to speak to someone about REO properties. Or call your real estate agent. Many agencies list REO properties, having established a business relationship with local lenders. Sometimes, buying through an agent can raise the price you ultimately pay for the property; after all, the agent is responsible to the bank to get a fair price for the home and is motivated to sell for a good price by the commission he or she stands to receive from the seller (the lender in this case).

Many real estate agents are eager to sell REO properties because in most cases the purchaser intends to resell the property after making repairs or upgrades. If your agent sells you the property, he may also gain the listing when you flip it. A smart agent is also eager to sell REO properties in the hopes of establishing exclusive listing arrangements with lenders—in other words, earning the right to list all the lender's REO properties. A good real estate agent is eager to find investor clients and a steady source of listings, and REO properties can help them develop both.

Tip: You can make your offer to purchase an REO property contingent on the lender offering financing. Ask the lender selling the property to provide financing; if the lender won't, your contract is invalid.

In some cases, lenders will jump at the chance to provide financing, especially on properties they have carried in inventory for a long period of time. Many lenders will not only provide financing but also offer lower rates or better terms. Why? As we've said before, the lender has a vested interest in reducing its REO inventory. Converting an REO property into a loan that brings in regular monthly payments is a win-win for the lender: It has converted a liability into an asset and improved its balance sheet. Many will offer financing at their lowest rates, especially if they intend to keep the loan in-house and not offer it on the secondary market.

Don't assume that lenders will jump at the chance to finance the purchase of their REO properties, especially if you don't have a solid track record of profitable foreclosure investments. When you are first starting out, you are probably better off securing your own financing before approaching a bank to buy REO properties. Pay cash for the first few properties and prove that you can do a good job with them. Once you're well established and have built a strong relationship with the bank, then you can pitch them on the idea of financing future investments in REO properties.

MYTH # **23**

Real Estate Agents Always Have First Crack at the Good Deals.

Fact: You Can Access Any Information Available to a Real Estate Agent

Foreclosures are public knowledge. You already have ready access to all the information available, and real estate agents don't have the inside track. The only way an agent has an advantage is if she has already developed a solid network of real estate professionals who can help her act quickly on potential opportunities. Fortunately, you can develop the same network by building your own team.

In fact, in some ways, agents are at a major disadvantage. If you're a part-time real estate investor, all you have to do is focus on finding good deals in your spare time. A real estate agent has to focus on listing properties, marketing properties, working with potential buyers, and attending closings. A successful agent is an incredibly *busy* agent.

Think about it this way. Say you're interested in a new home. You contact an agent and ask to be shown properties that meet your price range, your family's needs, with the amenities you want, and so on. First the agent must find suitable properties for you to view. Then, since you probably work during the day, you are only available to view properties at night or on the weekends. And you're not the only client the agent has, so in all likelihood the agent spends most days working with clients, preparing for closings, and talking to lenders, and most evenings and weekends showing properties, preparing offers, and handling the incredible amounts of paperwork and clerical tasks to support these activities. And since you want your new home to be perfect, you may need to look at 10 or even 20 homes before you can make a decision—and some of those homes you may look at two, three, or even four times.

Good agents are very busy working with existing clients, and at the same time must focus on finding new clients, since without new clients the agent's business—and income—will dry up.

There are a *lot* of deals out there! Don't let the thought of real estate agents beating you to an opportunity be a deterrent. While it is true that you may occasionally compete with a real estate agent for a foreclosure opportunity, it's much more likely you'll be competing with real estate investors like yourself.

 Most investors soon realize that the market holds many more opportunities than they have the time, energy, and resources to pursue. The same is true for real estate agents. By connecting with an agent who also invests in foreclosures, you are working with someone who knows how to do it and probably has more opportunities than he or she has the resources to pursue. Let this real estate agent list your homes when you're ready to sell, and the agent will be more likely to share leads on good foreclosure opportunities.

MYTH # **24**

I Can Find Better Deals Outside My Own Area.

Fact: You Maximize Your Profit Potential and Minimize Your Risk by Investing in Areas Where You Are More Familiar with the Housing Market

The best opportunities are where you live: You know the market, the property values, and the right people to help you succeed.

Most investors like to be close to their properties, because it shortens their travels and lets them use their time more efficiently. If you're making cosmetic repairs to a property you've purchased, wouldn't it be nice if it were only 10 minutes away from where you live?

Just as importantly, you'll develop expert knowledge about property values and real estate trends in your area. You'll know what properties are selling for in your area, and you'll more quickly be able to determine what you're willing to pay for a particular property. And you'll be able to develop a team of local professionals to help you—a team you can call on again and again. (Purchasing a property in another area may require you to find a different title company, contractors, attorneys, etc. Why waste time putting a new team together?)

Every day, properties enter the foreclosure process. While there may be great opportunities in other areas, there are great opportunities in your area, too, and you'll have a better feel for which neighborhoods have investment potential. You'll know whether:

♦ New homes are under construction.
♦ Owners are adding to the value of their homes by making repairs, additions, and landscaping improvements.
♦ Yards are well-kept and streets are clean and litter free.
♦ Shopping, parks, and commutes are convenient.
♦ Crime rates are low and the area is relatively safe.
♦ The schools have a good reputation.
♦ New industries are moving in, bringing new growth and opportunities.

Real estate trends change constantly. You could decide to buy a foreclosure property in a lower-middle-class area of town because you know young professionals are moving in and real estate values are on the rise. By knowing your area, you'll see, recognize, and profit from those trends—and you'll know which areas to avoid.

In addition to helping you make better investment decisions, investing in your own neighborhood can be very rewarding. Neighborhoods with lots of vacant properties can transform into crime-ridden slums almost overnight. By buying, fixing up, and selling foreclosures, you ensure that abandoned homes do not fall into disrepair, you encourage new families to move in, and you keep the riff-raff out. As your neighbors see the good you are doing, they will probably be more open to approaching you in the event that they fall into the foreclosure trap.

MYTH # **25**

Foreclosed Properties Are Always Trashed and Need Extensive and Costly Repairs.

Fact: For Every "Horror" Story, There's a "Move-In" Condition Story

It is true that some foreclosure properties are in poor condition. If you purchase the property at auction, you're buying as is and often without the opportunity to make even a brief inspection. You may have gotten a look at the exterior, but the condition of the interior of the home is usually a complete unknown. We had one property that required four dumpsters just to get the trash out of the first floor!

Other foreclosure properties may be in excellent condition. Bad things do happen to good people, and the homeowners, through no fault of their own, may lose their house due to illness, a job loss, or some other unexpected occurrence. Financially distressed homeowners are often otherwise responsible and caring individuals who treat their homes with care and would never consider damaging them in any way. (After all, if you lost your home in foreclosure, would you trash it?)

Of course, others will completely strip a property of any valuable asset, including the kitchen sink! You just need to be prepared and do your research.

Experienced and cautious auction buyers assume they will have to make at least some repairs: Replace the carpet, repaint the interior, replace at least a few of the appliances, and make upgrades to the kitchen and bathrooms. An investor we know has bought dozens of foreclosure properties and has almost always replaced the carpet and painted the walls. It was built right into the budget.

Experienced investors also understand they may have to make major repairs and improvements. Any investor who has purchased more than a few foreclosure auction properties has experienced some form of a horror story. (Remember, we're discussing auction properties; if you purchased a pre-foreclosure property or REO property, you had the chance to inspect the property prior to purchase, so there should be no major surprises.)

Sometimes the house is in poor shape simply due to neglect, while other times willful destruction occurs. Occasionally investors find properties where walls were trashed, appliances removed, toilets and sinks torn out, and thousands of dollars of work and significant amounts of time were required to return the house to marketable condition. Homeowners may resent moving out of foreclosed properties and can express that resentment in a physical way.

How do you mitigate the risk? One way is to focus on pre-foreclosure or REO purchases, since you'll have the chance to inspect the property thoroughly. Another is to make sure your auction walk-away price is low enough that you can still afford to make significant improvements or repairs if a worst-case scenario becomes a reality.

One more way to protect your investment is to insure it. Most insurance companies will not issue you a homeowner's policy on a property you purchased in foreclosure, but by paying extra, you can purchase other forms of insurance that protect the value of the property. Of course, the insurance agent will drive by to make sure the place isn't obviously damaged already, but if you have a policy in place and then the homeowners gut the house on their way out, your policy can help you recover from the loss.

If you expect the worst and factor that into your financial evaluation, you'll come out okay regardless of what a resentful or negligent homeowner may do.

To encourage homeowners to leave the property in good repair when they vacate the premises, offer them some extra cash in exchange for their leaving the home broom clean. *Broom clean* means that the homeowners will not damage or steal anything that is part of the home; they will take all their belongings with them; they will throw away anything they no longer want; and they will sweep and vacuum the house. You might even consider hiring a roll-off trash container for their use. Don't give them all the money until they are on their way out the door and have left the home in suitable condition.

For a true foreclosure property, make sure to check the *hidden* systems that can cost you a bundle, such as well and septic systems. Check the county health department records for a history—such information is available to the public.

MYTH # **26**

Something Else Is Wrong with the Property If It Was in Foreclosure.

Fact: Foreclosures Are Solely Due to the Owner's Inability to Meet Financial Commitments

Foreclosure is devastating for homeowners. Besides the loss of their home, their credit rating and their financial reputation suffer. Willingly choosing foreclosure is extremely rare, because the consequences are so severe.

Even if, for example, there is an existing problem with the house—say a structural issue, or a major expense such as the need to replace a furnace—why would the homeowner choose foreclosure? Again, the consequences are too severe. Often the homeowner would be better off, in the long run, selling the property rather than losing it through foreclosure.

It can be tempting to assume there are other reasons why the house is in foreclosure. Neighbors can gossip, co-workers can spread their opinions, and "knowledgeable" people can weigh in with their views, but unless the information comes from a trusted member of your team, disregard it. Do your homework, follow your instincts, make an informed evaluation of the investment potential, and don't assume that you or anyone else knows "why they're in foreclosure." The answer, almost always, is simply because the homeowners couldn't meet their financial commitments. Don't get caught up in speculation or gossip; spend your time on tasks that can help you be successful. If you truly have good reason to believe there's a major problem with a property, try to make an inspection ahead of time; if you can't, then move on and focus on purchasing another property. There are always more opportunities out there.

Although few families choose to trash their homes, many home-owners in foreclosure don't have the time and money to properly maintain the property. When you can't afford your house payments, you're probably not going to hire someone to repair the gutters, replace the windows, and install new carpeting. You can expect the home to be in some degree of disrepair, so even if it looks great on the outside, if you can't get inside to look around, leave something in your budget to cover the unexpected.

MYTH # **27**

I Don't Need an Inspection.

Fact: You Should Always at Least Inspect All Four Sides of the Exterior of the Home

While you can't gain access to the interior of the home without the homeowner's permission, you *can* get a fair idea of the condition of the interior by inspecting the condition of the exterior. At the very least, you should always walk around the property (without stepping onto the actual property, of course, unless invited) and get as close a look as possible of the exterior. Whenever you perform a walk-around evaluation, make sure to bring a notepad and a camera. Take thorough notes on the:

- General condition of the outside of the property
- Condition of the paint or siding
- Condition of the roof, gutters, and downspouts
- Condition of the windows and doors
- Condition of the yard (especially the property's "curb appeal," or the first impression it makes from the street)

If you don't have any home repair or construction experience, that's okay. The point of your walk-around inspection isn't to spot every possible defect; your goal at this point is to get a general impression of the condition of the property, noting "deferred maintenance," and to decide whether it's worth pursuing.

Take extensive notes about everything you see and use your camera to take photographs. Over the course of your real estate investment career you'll look at a lot of properties, and your notes can serve as a valuable reference down the road. It'll get hard to remember the details about every one.

Now take a walk around the property. You may not be able to see everything, but if you can, note:

+ The appearance of the backyard
+ The presence and condition of the garage or any other buildings
+ The condition of the exterior (paint, siding, roof, windows, doors, etc.)
+ The condition of any fences, gazebos, or other structures

Your main goal is to assess the property, but it also helps to get an overall feel for the neighborhood. So take time to look at nearby properties. Are they in good condition? Are there a lot of vacant properties or FOR SALE signs in the area, meaning you may have trouble selling? Do the owners appear to be taking care of their homes? Does the neighborhood feel safe? Are there any negative factors, like nearby major highways, manufacturing plants, or excessive traffic?

In some cases, your walk-around inspection will automatically disqualify a property from consideration. If the exterior is in disrepair, it's likely the interior is in poor shape, too. If the exterior is well maintained and cared for, it's likely the interior is in similar condition.

Don't automatically assume that you can't get a peek inside the home. The owners are certainly under no obligation to welcome you into their home, but if you approach them about purchasing during pre-foreclosure, you may get invited inside.

In some cases, the property may be unoccupied, and you can look through the windows and doors. (But don't go inside, even if the door is unlocked.) And if you do decide to peek in a few windows, it's a good idea to walk next door and let the neighbors know who you are and what you're doing. Aside from being the courteous and prudent thing to do, the neighbor may also offer information that is helpful: how long the property has been vacant, where the owners now live, why they moved away, the condition of the interior, and so on.

We have a saying, "Our eyes or no buys." Don't rely on what the homeowners tell you about the condition of the property, and don't send someone else out to inspect the property for you. You need to see the property with your own eyes, from all four sides, in order to have a clear image in your mind of the property's actual condition. Many novice investors looking for no-hassle investment opportunities get seriously burned when they buy properties site unseen.

MYTH # **28**

I Can't Get Inside, So There's No Way for Me to Estimate the Property Value.

Fact: Your Agent Can Help You Estimate the Fair Market Value, and You Can Apply a Standard Amount for New Paint, Carpet, and Cosmetic Repairs

If you can't look inside, your agent can still help you estimate the fair market value of the property by comparing it to similar homes in the same neighborhood and giving you a rough estimate of the property's square footage. Your agent can also assess the property's curb appeal and exterior condition to help make a value estimate. You can then estimate the cost of making common repairs: replacing carpet, painting all walls, and making miscellaneous repairs. To get estimates, call local painters, carpet distributors, and contractors. (Hopefully you already have some of these individuals on your team.) Explain the project and ask them to estimate the cost.

Some may be hesitant to give you an estimate based on limited information because they may be concerned you will later try to hold them to that price. Explain that you're simply trying to assess the opportunity and that if you purchase the property you will ask them to make a formal estimate. Be sure they understand that you need only a ballpark figure rather than a precise and formal proposal.

Now work backwards. You have the real estate agent's estimate of property value. We'll use that figure as the price at which you hope to sell the property. Subtract the agent's commission (6%) from the sale price. Then subtract the total cost of repairs, along with the cost of holding the property: mortgage payments, taxes, insurance, and so forth. (Your agent can help you determine those estimated costs, or you can talk to your lender.) The resulting number is the most you should be willing to pay for the property, if you're willing to break even. (Visit GetFlipping.com for a purchase price estimator that performs the calculations for you.)

If you are unable to inspect the interior, there may be surprises. Experienced investors add a contingency amount to their estimated costs for unanticipated expenses. You may decide to add $10,000 to your costs, or 10% of the sales price, or more. Each investor applies a different contingency, but here's a rule of thumb: The less cash you have on hand, the higher your contingency figure should be; that way you're less likely to find yourself needing to make repairs you can't afford.

Since you wish to make a profit and not merely break even, now determine how much you wish to make. Some investors hope for a 20% return, others for 30%. The amount of profit you wish to make is a function of your goals, the amount of time you'll need to spend on the project, and, frankly, what a realistic return will be. (Don't expect to buy every foreclosure property for $50,000 and sell them for $500,000. In other words, some properties will be home runs—others will be bunt singles.)

Here's an example. Say your agent estimates the fair market value of a property to be $200,000. You estimate your holding and sales cost will be a total of $18,000. You also estimate you'll need to spend $10,000 on repairs and upgrades. To be safe, you decide to add $10,000 in contingency costs. The most you can pay, in order to break even, is $162,000. You hope to make $10,000 on the transaction, so your walk-away price is $152,000; if you can purchase the property for less, you lower your risk and potentially increase your profits.

Overestimate costs, underestimate profits. This will provide you with an additional buffer, which is especially important for when you are first getting started. Over time, you will hone your skill at being able to estimate property values for yourself.

MYTH # **29**

Never Bid on a Second Mortgage.

Fact: Bidding on a Second Mortgage Is Usually a Bad Idea for Beginners, but as You Gain Experience, You May Benefit—as Long as You Buy the First Mortgage, Too

First a little background. When you buy a property at a foreclosure auction, what you're really doing is buying a mortgage. The first mortgage is called the *senior lien* and gives the buyer the most control over the property. Other claims against the property, like home equity loans, are called *junior liens*. (The term *second mortgage* is normally used to refer to an equity loan, but *junior liens* is the more accurate term because some properties can have a number of liens against them.) The senior lien is the most important lien, because often during the foreclosure process junior liens are wiped out. For more about the hierarchy of liens, see Myth #21.

That's why researching the title is so critical, and why having a good title company on your team is so important. Unless the homeowner just took out another loan using the property as collateral, records should be available at your Register of Deeds office showing all of the liens against the home. Your title company can generate a *title commitment* that also contains a complete list of all the liens against the property and may be a little easier for you to decipher than trying to sort through the records at the Register of Deeds office.

Remember, if you're buying a junior lien, you aren't buying the property. You're buying the right to collect that lien if funds are available after the auction sale. You may make a profit without having to take possession of the property, or you might find yourself out your entire investment. You also may be out your investment if someone else buys a lien that's higher up the pecking order.

Here's the bottom line: Don't buy a junior lien without buying the senior lien *and* paying any overdue taxes (the property tax lien or deed trumps *any* other liens!). That way you control the property and don't have to worry about other lien holders taking precedence. Before you consider investing in junior liens, make sure you have experience buying senior liens, and make sure you have a good title company and an experienced attorney on your side to help you.

 You can often buy a second mortgage directly from the lien holder for less than you can purchase it at an auction (since it may be virtually worthless after the foreclosure sale). Remind the lien holder that once the first mortgage is sold at auction, the lien holder stands to have its lien wiped off the books by the foreclosure. By accepting whatever you're willing to offer, the lien holder gets at least something out of the deal. This could save you thousands on the acquisition while enabling the junior lien holder to walk away with at least a little money in their pocket.

Analyzing the Deal

Once you've narrowed down your list of acceptable properties, then it becomes crucial to look at other aspects of the deal and decide whether you're ready to pull the trigger. This is the stage in the process that is most exciting and also most dreadful for novice investors. You want to make a decision, buy the property, and start working on fixing it up, but you don't want to pay too much and destine yourself to losing money.

In this section, we try to remove some of the fear and trepidation that could convince you not to pull the trigger. After all, you've gotten this far, and if you have done your homework, you should be able to confidently present your offer to the homeowners or start bidding at your first auction. Here we blast away at some of the most common myths associated with the structure of the foreclosure deal.

MYTH # **30**

I Found the Opportunity Too Late—There's Not Enough Time.

Fact: It's Never Too Late as Long as You Have Time to Research the Neighborhood, Estimate Value and Costs, and Ensure the Deal Makes Sense

Jumping into a pool without making sure it's full of water is foolish. So is failing to perform due diligence, but almost every experienced investor can share stories about quickly leaping into a deal that sounded too good to be true—and was. It's easy to get excited and pull the trigger on the "deal of a lifetime" because the opportunity is just too good to pass up.

Chip remembers once such deal early on in Ann Arbor, Michigan. There was a frenzy building up between several parties looking at this abandoned house, which appeared in every respect to be a pretty good deal. Structurally it was fine; it needed some paint and repairs, but could be turned around fairly quickly. He jumped on it, only to find later that because of the time it had been vacant, it had been *condemned* by the city. Moving too quickly cost him time and dollars. A couple of quick phone calls could have saved months of red tape and expense.

To safeguard themselves, many investors impose an artificial time limit on themselves. We know an investor who refuses to even consider evaluating an opportunity if the property auction is one week away or less; he feels he needs at least that much time to determine its value, estimate repair and holding costs, and then sleep on the decision.

It's smart to find ways to keep emotion out of your decisions. Real estate investing is a business; as a friend likes to say, "You may love the deal, but the deal can't love you back." But speed is often of the essence, especially in areas where you face competition from other investors. How do you act quickly and yet make rational and objective decisions?

Experience is a critical factor, and so is developing a process for evaluating opportunities. (We'll talk about how to analyze opportunities starting in Myth #36.) The more familiar you are with your area, the quicker you'll be able to estimate property value. (That's one reason why the grass is never greener on the other side of your area's fence.) Experienced investors who keep up with local trends and market conditions can often estimate a property's value from the curb—to within 5% or so. If you're inexperienced, your real estate agent can help you estimate a property's value. And as your experience grows, you'll develop your *own* ballpark estimates for repairing and renovating a property. An investor friend of ours uses $7 per square foot when he is estimating repair costs for properties he can't inspect; he assumes that a 2,000-square-foot home will need $14,000 in repairs to get it ready for resale.

Too late is really just a function of how much time you need to thoroughly analyze the opportunity. If you don't have time to estimate value, estimate repair costs, and line up financing, among other tasks, then, yes, it is too late, and it's time to move on to the next deal. If you can put together estimates that you're comfortable with and perform your due diligence, and you already have your financing in place, then it's not too late to spot and capitalize on a great opportunity.

 Sometimes homeowners may run out of time to pursue a particular option; for example, homeowners who decide that they want to reinstate their loan the night before the sale may not have time to get the money together. By having cash on hand or at least having quick access to cash, you can buy time for the homeowners to work with you. For example, you can loan them the money to reinstate their mortgage, so they can sell the property to you. Or, you can buy the property at auction and then sell it back to them for a reasonable profit. In other words, it is often too late for the homeowners, but not too late for you.

MYTH # **31**

I Found the Opportunity Too Early—I'll Probably Waste My Time.

Fact: The Earlier You Discover the Opportunity, the Greater Your Chance of Eventually Purchasing the Property

You can spend a great deal of time researching a property and working with homeowners in pre-foreclosure only to lose out on the opportunity to purchase the home. The homeowners can decide to reinstate, for example. Another investor can buy the home right out from under you. Or numerous other things can occur to derail your efforts to acquire the home. Don't let that deter you, though; even if you spent hours analyzing a deal that doesn't go through, you have still gained experience and developed additional expertise. Developing knowledge and skill is *never* a waste of time.

More importantly, some of the best deals are available in pre-foreclosure. If you've contacted the homeowner early in the foreclosure process and offered to purchase the property, not only have you helped the homeowner out of an incredibly difficult situation, but you've also minimized the competition from other investors. And if you aren't able to purchase it in pre-foreclosure, you probably did at least get the opportunity to inspect the property thoroughly. As a result you have the ability to develop an accurate figure for repair costs, rather than simply estimating based on experience, which helps you set a precise walk-away price when you attend the foreclosure auction.

In our opinion, the earlier you enter the process the better: You can purchase in pre-foreclosure, you have plenty of time to bring in your team to help you assess the deal, and you have time to arrange financing and pull together the cash you may need. Worst case: If the foreclosure doesn't go through, you've gained experience—and experience for investors is priceless.

 The more you know about a property, the better able you are to develop an accurate estimate of how much to pay for it. By getting involved early in the process, you immediately begin gathering information. You know the situation the homeowners are in, what they would like out of the deal, what the lien holders stand to lose or gain, and what the homeowners are doing or not doing to save their home and secure their equity. This knowledge puts you in a better position to wheel and deal and make an offer when the time is right.

MYTH # **32**

I Can't Get a Good Deal Through a Real Estate Agent.

Fact: As Long as the Seller Is Highly Motivated and Willing to Make a Deal, You Can Still Find Great Deals on Pre-Foreclosures If the Homeowner Is Selling Through an Agent

Financially distressed homeowners facing foreclosure have limited options if they want to hang onto what's left of their credit and any equity they have in the home. One option is to sell the property—normally in a hurry. While many will not consider selling their home in pre-foreclosure unless contacted by someone like you, others will recognize that their options are limited and list the property through a real estate agent. If you are in a position to close quickly, you have a distinct advantage over other interested parties.

You also have the chance to buy at below market value. Let's say the average home in your area stays on the market for five months. (As we write this, in some areas the average home stays on the market for around 12 months.) Let's also assume that to avoid foreclosure, the homeowners need to sell their home in less than two months. One factor of how long a home takes to sell is price; as a rule of thumb, homes priced below market value sell more quickly, homes priced at market value sell close to the area's average time on market, and those priced above market value can sit, seemingly forever. In order to sell this home quickly, the agent is likely to recommend pricing the home below market value. How far below is a function of the homeowner's need to sell the property, and how quickly.

Properties priced below market value tend to sell quickly, so you'll need to be able to act fast. Lining up financing ahead of time is critical. Spend time with your lender and ask what you can do to put yourself in a position to purchase a home as quickly as possible, and then take the steps that he or she recommends. At the very least, you should be preapproved for a loan amount that will cover the purchase price.

Also, don't be afraid to make an offer, even if it's significantly lower than the listing price. While offering $50,000 for a home listed at $200,000 is silly (and also insulting to the agent and the homeowner), if you offer 20 to 30% below the listing price, you may find your offer is accepted—as long as you can close quickly. If the foreclosure auction is coming up in, say, one month, you'll need to complete the transaction in a hurry. The auction will take place unless you and the homeowner can negotiate an extension with the lender's attorney.

If your lowball offer would require the owner to sell at a loss, the real estate agent may be able to negotiate a short sale with the lender that enables the homeowners to walk away free and clear of any debt. Lenders will rarely agree to a short sale that puts money in the seller's pocket, but they may be willing to accept less than the full balance due on the loan if they can get the bad loan off their books.

MYTH # **33**

I Can't Get a Good Deal from Bankruptcy.

Fact: The Price You Pay Depends on the Result of the Auction or Sale, Not on the Fact the Owners Went Bankrupt

Once bankruptcy is declared, in essence the property owners turn the house over to a court-appointed receiver or trustee—an attorney in charge of either liquidating the assets to pay off debts or restructuring the debt to formulate more reasonable payment plans. In some cases, homeowners can save their home in bankruptcy. Most of the time, however, the home is sold as an REO property or at a bankruptcy auction. So, like any other investment opportunity, whether you get a good deal or not depends on the value of the property and the price you can get it for.

Bankruptcy essentially shuts down the foreclosure process, at least temporarily. Homeowners facing foreclosure who declare bankruptcy buy time to restructure their finances and relieve the pressure from bill collectors and other creditors. At the same time, their assets are frozen; the assets are now considered to be part of the estate and must be sold to pay off outstanding creditors. A homeowner who enters bankruptcy no longer has the right to sell the property; if you were negotiating with the owner to buy the home in pre-foreclosure, that opportunity is now lost. From here on you'll be dealing with the bankruptcy court or the trustee for the estate.

Two main types of bankruptcy are available to homeowners. Let's take a quick look at each type:

1. **Chapter 7 Bankruptcy:** Homeowners filing Chapter 7 turn over control of all their assets to a court-appointed trustee. The trustee's

role is to liquidate assets to pay off claims against the estate (the homeowners). Claims can include unpaid mortgages, credit card debt, back taxes, or any other legal or financial obligations. If you want to purchase the home, your offer must be approved by the trustee.

2. **Chapter 13 Bankruptcy:** Homeowners filing Chapter 13 wish to restructure their debt, or in other words to make arrangements with their creditors to repay their obligations. While the process of restructuring debt may mean that some assets—including the home—will be sold, in other cases, creditors agree that the debt will be paid off over a longer period of time. If you want to purchase the home, you'll work directly with the homeowner's attorney. Any deal will then have to be approved by the court.

You can purchase the home at various stages of the bankruptcy process:

◆ **Before the bankruptcy filing:** As long as the homeowners have not filed for bankruptcy, you can purchase the home directly from them just like you would in any normal real estate transaction. Some homeowners will be motivated to offer you a great deal so they can afford bankruptcy; others who are considering filing may be unwilling to take less than fair market value. Since you may not know that the homeowners are even considering filing, don't worry about the possibility of bankruptcy at this stage; simply make an offer based on what you're willing to pay for the house.

◆ **Bankruptcy filed, but homeowners still in possession:** Once bankruptcy is filed, the homeowners remain in possession for a period of time and can accept offers and negotiate to sell the property. The attorney or trustee must notify creditors and they must approve the sale since they now have a vested interest in the proceedings. Because the creditors are involved, the odds are relatively slim that all parties will approve an offer that's below market value.

◆ **Property in liquidation:** Control of the property is eventually transferred to the trustee for liquidation. The trustee can usually select the best offer for the property. At this stage, creditors can object to the sale price, but the trustee can overrule those objections if he or she sees fit. (The trustee can also reject your offer and turn the property over to a creditor.) Your best chance for getting a good deal is at the liquidation stage, since the homeowners are no longer involved, the trustee is simply interested in selecting the best offer, and the creditors are motivated to get at least *some* of their money back.

- **Property has been liquidated:** If another investor purchases the property, your chances of buying it are effectively over. But, a creditor may buy or be given the property, and you may be able to purchase it from the creditor. While you may have to pay more than the creditor paid, the premium may be small, because many creditors would prefer to take a relatively low price to avoid the time, cost, and hassles of selling the property on their own.

As we mentioned before, buying bankruptcy properties takes experience and a great lawyer on your side. But great opportunities do exist, so once you gain experience you could find that you enjoy the complexity— and profits—to be found in bankruptcy investing.

If you're working with homeowners, and they mention a desire to consult with a bankruptcy attorney (or an attorney of any kind), do not try to discourage them from doing so. It could get you into serious legal trouble. Simply let the homeowners know that if the bankruptcy option does not work out for them, you are willing to continue working with them.

MYTH # **34**

I Can't Get a Good Deal on a Government REO.

Fact: Of Course You Can: Simply Estimate the Value, Determine Your Walk-Away Price, and *Never* Pay Too Much

The Department of Housing and Urban Development (HUD), the Department of Veterans Affairs (VA), and other government agencies sell seized or surplus real estate. The Internal Revenue Service (IRS) is the most active seller of government REO properties since many homes are seized due to tax liens or tax defaults.

Each agency has its own rules and regulations for sales. Companies such as Ocwen have contracted with government agencies (in Ocwen's case, with the VA) to manage and sell their properties. To learn more, visit the following web sites:

- **Internal Revenue Service:** www.treas.gov/auctions/irs
- **Dept of Housing and Urban Development:** www.hud.gov/homes/homesforsale.cfm
- **Homes for Sale by the U.S. Government:** www.homesales.gov
- **Federal Deposit Insurance Corporation:** www.fdic.gov/buying/index.html
- **Small Business Administration:** www.sba.gov/assets.html
- **Ocwen:** www.ocwen.com
- **U.S. Customs Seizures:** www.treas.gov/auctions/customs/realprop.html
- **USDA Real Estate for Sale:** www.resales.usda.gov

You can purchase government-owned properties through designated real estate agents or by bidding at auction.

First-time homebuyers often finance their homes with FHA-insured loans. If the property owner fails to make mortgage payments, the FHA initiates foreclosure proceedings and eventually resells the homes through a HUD-registered real estate agent. HUD homes are typically lower-end homes because they're owned by first-time homeowners. You can often find clean, well-maintained homes, but you won't find a high-end property. They often sell for close to market value, so the chances of making a tremendous profit are relatively low. HUD properties are also sold as is, although you will be given the opportunity to make a complete inspection.

HUD homes are owner occupied: That means you'll be required to sign a contract stating you'll live in the home for at least 12 months before selling it. If you're interested in flipping for a quick profit, HUD properties are not for you. On the other hand, you may qualify for FHA financing and possibly a low-interest loan if you are purchasing and renovating a rundown property. One such FHA first-time homeowner REO program allows you to get in for only $100! (See www.HUD.gov for link to listings.)

Repossessed VA properties are also resold on the open market by VA-registered real estate agents. While you don't have to be a military veteran to purchase a home from the VA, you will need to agree to live in the home for 12 months.

Homes are also lost when the homeowners fail to pay their taxes: The taxing authority eventually seizes the property, sells it at auction, and uses the proceeds to recover the taxes owed. Tax sales are typically handled by the sheriff's office, county treasurer, or sometimes even the state. Your real estate attorney can give you information, or you can visit your sheriff's office or treasurer's office for details on how the process works in your area.

You can also buy properties from the Internal Revenue Service. When a property is foreclosed on, the IRS typically releases any lien it has on the property. Whoever buys the senior lien must give the IRS 30 days' notice in case the IRS wishes to redeem the property and sell it to recover the taxes owed, but the IRS normally does not do so. In some cases, the IRS will take possession of the property, which means it will have to be sold at auction.

IRS auctions are typically handled by mail. You can see properties for sale on the IRS web site and get details about how to bid. If you are the winning bidder, you will need to submit 20% of the purchase price as a down payment, with the remainder due in 30 days. The homeowners also have four months to redeem the property.

You can find good deals on government-owned homes. Thoroughly inspect the home, use comparables and your real estate to determine the value, and do your homework. Regardless of whether it's a government-owned property, any deal you can profit on is a good deal. If you can't make a profit, it's not a good deal, so walk away and wait for the next one!

 To purchase as owner-occupied from HUD or the VA, some investors lie and claim that they fully intend to live in the home for the required 12-month period. We strongly discourage you from following this practice. They do check, and if they catch you in a lie, not only do you risk losing the home, but you can also face some stiff penalties and even jail time.

MYTH # **35**

I Can't Get a Good Deal from the Lender.

Fact: Lenders Will Frequently Cut Their Losses Instead of Carrying the Asset on Their Books for Months

Lenders don't want to be in the real estate business; as we mentioned earlier, they're legally required *not* to be in the real estate business. The lender wants to make loans and collect fees and payments. The lender doesn't let emotion enter the process, as a homeowner often will, and is likely to view the process objectively.

Since you have a good sense of the REO process from Myth #22, let's look at ways you can negotiate with the lender to get good deals on REO properties. But before we look at different strategies you can employ, let's discuss the basics of negotiating effectively.

Whenever you bid for a property, whether at auction or by making an offer, you should always calculate the maximum price you're willing to pay ahead of time. Unless you get access to new information, stick to your maximum price—don't fall prey to auction fever.

The lender's representative expects your initial offer to be a starting point and will usually treat it that way. Obviously, if you offer your final price right away, you'll have short-circuited the bargaining process and possibly will end up paying a higher price than necessary.

The lender's rep will probably be unimpressed with your first offer; after all, in negotiations, it's her job to act unimpressed. Move your bid up, but do so in increments. If the property is sold to someone else while you're negotiating, don't worry. There will be other opportunities.

Lender's reps may also be required to report the stages of negotiations to their superior in order to show they did everything possible to get the best price. Accepting your first bid will not create the perception that the rep is a tough negotiator; that's another reason to expect your early offers to be denied.

A basic negotiating tactic is to eventually "split the difference" in bids. (Believe it or not, studies show that a majority of the time the final sale price will be approximately halfway between the *asking price* and the *initial offer*, no matter how outrageous one or both of those two amounts may be.) Never split the difference unless that amount falls under your predetermined maximum price.

If you don't reach agreement, thank the rep for considering your offer, explain that you're unable to go higher, and ask that your name be kept on file. If the lender doesn't get other offers, you may hear from the rep at a later date. Time works against the lenders, since every day they hold the property costs them money—and lenders have a thorough understanding of the time value of money.

You can also ask to submit a written offer to be placed in the lender's files. That way the lender can contact you if it decides to accept your offer. The lender often rejects offers that come early in the process in hopes of receiving higher offers; when higher offers don't arrive, the lender will often accept your previously rejected offer.

Be persistent. Don't expect the lender to keep in contact with you. The person handling the sale in all likelihood has a number of other duties. By staying in touch, you may be able to reach a compromise price that satisfies the lender's needs and gains you a valuable investment property.

Now let's look at different methods for making offers.

Single Offers. The most common way to bid on REO properties is to make a bid on one property. Find a property you're interested in and make an offer. You'll negotiate and eventually either purchase the property or not. In essence it's like a normal real estate transaction between two individuals, but in this case one "individual" is the lender. In all other respects it's really the same and can carry the same contingencies, such as home inspection requirements, contingencies for obtaining financing, and so forth.

If you're new to REO investing or to real estate investing in general, this is the best way to go. Nothing is more valuable than experience, and bidding on individual properties will give you experience both in the buying process and, if your bid is accepted, in the process of repairing, renovating, and reselling investment properties.

Note: Make sure you always include the provision in your contract that your offer is dependent on obtaining suitable financing. Doing so benefits you in two ways: (1) If you can't obtain financing, you are released from the contract, and (2) the lender may decide to offer financing to you at favorable terms in order to finalize the sale of a property.

Multiple Offers. You can also make multiple offers on different properties at the same time using separate contracts. The advantage to this approach is clear: If you have one property you're extremely interested in, you make an offer on that property and enter negotiations, but you may not win the bidding. In the meantime, a second property you would have been willing to invest in could have been sold, causing you to miss another opportunity. Creating separate contracts on multiple properties allows you to "hedge your bets" and expands your purchase opportunities.

Doing so also creates some risk, especially if you bid on multiple prop-erties but can't afford to actually purchase them all. If all the contracts are accepted, you have a problem. There are two ways to avoid this.

The first is simply to make all your offers contingent on obtaining suit-able financing. Let's say you've put contracts on three separate properties. Unless you have the financial assets to actually qualify for financing for all three, qualifying for financing on one may be all you're eligible for, causing the other two contracts to be invalid. (Effectively you've ensured you won't have to purchase all three, even though you did bid on them.)

There's a problem with this approach, though, even though it can be effective. Your goal is to establish a long-term relationship with the lender's REO department so you'll possibly get advance notice of properties for sale. You'll also establish yourself as a credible and reputable buyer, which can help you during negotiations or when you're competing with another party for a house. At the very least, the REO department will be irritated with your approach since they may have stopped marketing the house or houses you didn't end up qualifying for. Creating a financing contingency on multiple properties you have no ability to purchase may be an effective short-term technique, but it will not help you in the long run, and is not a professional way to conduct business.

A better way to handle making multiple offers with separate contracts is to be up front and open about your intentions. Include a contingency stating you're making offers on, for instance, three different houses, but you'll only be willing to actually purchase one (or two) of the three. To protect yourself, you can also include a contingency for obtaining financing for those two houses. This way the lender knows ahead of time you aren't interested in purchasing all three; they'll appreciate your candor, and they'll understand why you're making multiple bids. And you'll have created a positive, professional impression that can help you establish a long-term business relationship.

One Offer on Multiple Properties. Some investors create investment groups made up of multiple investors; they pool their assets (and talents) for the purposes of buying REO properties.

If you or your partners have the financial resources, you can make a *blanket* offer on a collection of different properties. The major advantage to this approach is that you're likely to pay a lower total price for all the properties than you would if you had purchased them individually. Why? The lender may be delighted to dispose of a number of properties and will therefore willingly reduce the total price. Plus, the more properties you purchase, the lower the risk you face of any one property requiring extensive repairs and investment. In effect, you spread your risk like you would by diversifying stock market investments.

You should always perform due diligence on each of the properties. Just because your overall risk is minimized doesn't mean you shouldn't attempt to know as much as possible about the investment potential of each property. The best way to minimize risk is to do your homework.

You always want to negotiate from a position of strength. To strengthen your position as an investor, have cash or access to it before presenting your offer, do what you say you're going to do, and know what you want before you ask for it. REO managers do not have time to waste on people who simply want to test the waters and pretend to be investors. They have a problem they need to deal with: a bad loan and a home they don't want. Your job is to solve their problem and earn a decent amount of money for doing so.

MYTH # **36**

The Purchase Price and My Fix-Up Costs Are the Only Costs I Need to Consider.

Fact: There Are a Number of Costs You Should Evaluate—Including Your Time

Let's say you look at a foreclosure property and think, for example, "*Hmm* ... if I pay $200,000 for this house, put $20,000 in improvements into it, and sell for $250,000, I'll make $30,000!"

You would be wrong. As you've already seen, you also need to consider closing costs, payments and fees, taxes, utilities, interest payments, and the cost of selling the house and closing on *that* sale, too.

Before we consider costs, let's take another quick look at determining the purchase price. One of the challenges you face when looking at investment property is not only to assess the current value of the property but also to assess its potential future value. Why? You want to buy the property at a price below its current market potential. Remember, any property is worth exactly what a buyer is prepared to pay for it—no more and no less. As a buyer of a foreclosure property, you set the value of the property when you purchased it. The question you have to answer—and this determines your profit potential— is, "Does this property have potential and can it be changed in ways to attract another buyer to pay more for the property than I did?" That difference in value, minus your costs, is your profit. A house is not worth the tax assessment value or the appraisal value: A house is only worth what a willing, ready, and able buyer will agree to pay *and* you are willing to sell it for.

Now let's look at costs. We'll use a theoretical property and round numbers to make the math easier. We weren't able to inspect the interior of the property, so we used 10% as our estimate of repair costs. We also assumed we'll pay a 6% commission to our real estate agent for selling the home when we flip it.

Estimated Value (after improvements)	**$200,000.00**
Closing Costs (at purchase)	$3,000.00
Holding Costs	$5,000.00
Repairs	$20,000.00
Back Taxes Due (if applicable)	$1,500.00
Contingency	$5,000.00
Total Expenses	**$33,500.00**
Real Estate Commission (at sale)	$12,000.00
Closing Costs (at sale)	$2,000.00
Total Costs of Sale	**$14,000.00**
Total Cash Out	**$47,500.00**
Breakeven Purchase Price	**$152,500.00**

If the entire transaction goes as planned and we pay $152,500 for the house, we'll break even. But we're not doing all this work and putting our money at risk to break even, are we? While we're at it, let's factor in profit. We like to shoot for at least a 20% profit; that way if unexpected expenses do pop up, we have some margin before we lose money on the deal. (And if we sell the house for more than we expected, or our expenses are lower, we make an even better return.)

We adjust our profit percentage based on current market conditions. If the market is hot, the likelihood you'll get your price for the house is high; in down markets, you may need to factor in a higher profit percentage in order to hit your 20% target (in case prices continue to drop). Use this breakdown to determine which percentage to use:

Divide Market Value By:

Values are rising	1.20
Values are steady	1.25
Values are declining	1.30

So, assuming an estimated market value of $200,000:

1.20	$166,666
1.25	$160,000
1.30	$153,846

In this case, we'll assume a steady real estate market, so we'll target a 25% profit, hopefully ensuring we'll make at least 20% if the market cools.

Estimated Value (after improvements)	**$200,000.00**
Adjusted Market Value (profit factored in)	$160,000.00
Closing Costs (at purchase)	$3,000.00
Holding Costs	$5,000.00
Repairs	$20,000.00
Back Taxes Due (if applicable)	$1,500.00
Contingency	$5,000.00
Total Expenses and Profit	**$73,500.00**
Real Estate Commission (at sale)	$12,000.00
Closing Costs (at sale)	$2,000.00
Total Costs of Sale	**$14,000.00**
Total Cash Out (excluding profit)	**$47,500.00**
Walk-Away Purchase Price	**$112,500.00**

Keep in mind there are at least two other costs we haven't discussed. The first is *opportunity cost*. Opportunity cost is the cost of pursuing one choice instead of another. Every investment you make has an opportunity cost. To use a non–real estate example, the opportunity cost of going to college is the money you would have earned if you worked instead. All other things considered equal (forgetting, for example, that maybe you want to go to college so you *don't* have to work for another four years), you lose four years of salary while getting your degree; on the other hand, you hope to earn more during your career thanks to your education to offset those lost wages.

Opportunity cost is not limited to monetary or financial costs: Lost time, lost recreation, or any other benefit can also be an opportunity cost. Investing in foreclosures takes time; one of the opportunity costs is the loss of some leisure time. (But if lost leisure time is a major concern to you, you probably wouldn't be reading this book.)

In real estate investing terms, opportunity cost boils down to making choices between opportunities. If you are considering two potential invest-ments and can only make *one*, which one is likely to generate the greatest return? Which fits best into your workload, your skill set, and the time you have available? If you invest in a property that can generate, at best, only a 4% return, you're probably better off keeping your money in the bank. If you can spend the same amount of time and money on a property that will generate a 20% return instead of another property that will yield only a 10% return, which would you choose?

The second major cost is *your time*. Successful investing, whether in stocks, bonds, old coins, art, or real estate, takes time. If you buy a foreclosure property and plan to do some repairs yourself, you will save money on repair costs but you'll also spend time. How much is your time worth? If you'll spend 300 hours repairing and renovating a property and will make $3,000 in profit, your time was worth $10 per hour. If that sounds good to you, great! If it doesn't, you'll need to adjust your cost estimates accordingly.

While we're talking about time, if you plan to make repairs yourself, make sure you have the time to do so. The longer it takes to prepare the property for sale, the longer you'll hold it, and the higher your holding costs will be. You may save, say, $1,000 by painting several rooms yourself, but if it takes you a month to complete, your additional holding costs will be significantly higher than the amount you saved.

 You can significantly reduce your holding costs by living in the house you flip, which is exactly what many real estate investors do when they are just starting out. Instead of chalking up your monthly expenses as holding costs, simply consider them rent. Another way to trim your holding costs is to price the property correctly the first time. By offering the best home in its class at the best price, you can sell the home faster and trim your holding costs enough to more than cover the cost of selling the home for a little less.

MYTH # **37**

I Should Adjust My Bidding Strategy Depending on How Many Bidders Show Up and How Eager They Seem to Be to Purchase the Property.

Fact: Base Your Bid on a Thorough Assessment of Value and Costs; No Other Considerations Really Matter

First, we'll repeat a rule you should live by: Set your walk-away price and *stick to it*. *Never* bid higher than your maximum or walk-away price.

Once you've determined your walk-away price, the strategy you use when bidding during a public auction depends on your personality and your willingness to try to outfox your competition. Here are some techniques you can try:

- **Bore the opposition into submission.** Outbid the highest bidder by the minimum amount allowed. For example, the referee may specify that bids must be in $50 increments. If so, keep bidding $50 higher than the highest bid—the other bidders may get bored or irritated and back out.

- **Jump in the deep end.** You can also open with a high bid to try to shock your competition. You may be able to scare off an inexperienced bidder or two. At the same time, you may pay a lot more than necessary for the property, because the bidding may not have reached the amount you bid. If you feel sure the property will sell for a lot more than your high opening gambit, give it a try—but never open with your maximum bid.

- **Be quiet and mysterious.** Softly announced and seemingly casual bids can give the impression of confidence and security. Some bidders may not even hear your bid, causing them to waste time and energy deciding who you are and what you're up to.

- **Be over the top.** Or, you can holler your bids out so everyone in the area knows your offer. It's unsettling for other bidders, but if you're shy or self-conscious, this may not be the strategy for you.

- **Bid unpredictably.** Most bidders follow a pattern, either raising each offer by a set amount or waiting until later in the process to begin bidding. If you bid several times, then drop out for a bit only to reenter later in the process, other bidders may be thrown off—they may have assumed you were already out of the running. Or consider exceeding the previous bid by $100 one time and $500 the next. Other bidders who feel you're a wildcard can become hesitant and unsure.

Keep in mind that if the other bidders are as objective and dispassionate as you are, no bidding strategy will outfox them. They, like you, will simply stop bidding once the price exceeds their own walk-away price. On the other hand, many bidders do not stay rational and can let their emotions get the best of them. If that's the case, a little gamesmanship can be the difference between winning and losing a property. Remember opportunity cost from Myth #36? If a competing bidder gets tied up in a property she bid too much for, she may not have the resources to compete against you when the next auction rolls around.

Before you even think about bidding, research several properties and prepare a detailed portfolio for each one, complete with your walk-away price. Attend the auctions for these homes and see what the outcome is. Did the bidding exceed your walk-away price? Were you pretty much on target with the price you would have been willing to pay? You might also consider following up with the investor who purchased the property to see what it ultimately sold for and how much money the investor sunk into the project (assuming, of course, that the person is willing to share this information).

MYTH # **38**

It Doesn't Matter Where It's Located; Since I'll Pay Well Below Market Value, the Location Isn't Important.

Fact: Location, Location, Location Applies to *All* Real Estate Deals

You've probably heard the saying that the three most important considerations in buying a property are location, location, location: If you buy well, you'll sell well. This truism is the cornerstone of every real estate investment strategy, and here's why.

In less desirable locations, the homes are cheaper and so-called "good deals" are relatively easy to find. (Why do we say "good deals"? Because a low price doesn't mean a good deal; a house selling for $40,000 may sound like a bargain, but it really may be worth only $40,000 or *less*.)

Many first-time homebuyers hope to find a home in need of minor repairs so they can buy cheap and sell for a handsome profit. True, fixing up a home for profit can work if you do your homework and handle the repairs wisely. Unfortunately, many people fall into the trap of adding onto or remodeling a small home and overimproving for the neighborhood. In the end, they have created a white elephant that takes a long time to sell and/or requires selling at a loss.

The better the location, the more you can improve both the house and its value. If the overall real estate market heats up, better areas appreciate more quickly. When the market cools, better locations tend to hold their value. In less desirable areas, you won't be able to get back your investment on anything other than basic improvements unless you buy significantly below market value.

For example, there are older neighborhoods in nearly every city with small 900-square-foot homes built in the 1940s and 1950s. If these neighborhoods are near a local college, parks, a thriving downtown, or other desirable locations, their value has probably soared. On the other hand, these same types of homes located near an airport or mall will sell for significantly less, and will be much harder to sell.

One of the largest factors contributing to the desirability of an area is the local school system. An area that has a reputation for good schools will tend to have more homebuyers actively seeking to move there. When homes are in attractive school districts, Realtors often advertise that fact, knowing they will attract more homebuyers.

A good area with desirable schools tends to create relatively rapid home appreciation. In a seller's market, these homes will appreciate faster; in a down market, they'll hold their value longer.

Here are some of the keys to a good location:

- It is close to colleges, upscale shopping, and cultural and sporting events. Homeowners in these areas tend to spend significant sums remodeling older homes.
- It is within one of the best school districts. (Don't know which areas have the best school systems? Your real estate agent can tell you.)
- It is close to where young professionals work and want to live. These are buyers you want interested in your properties.

- ◆ Houses stay on the market for a relatively short period of time.
- ◆ Reasonably priced starter homes are hard to find.

These factors can alert you to less desirable locations:

- ◆ Busy streets and traffic
- ◆ Houses poorly maintained
- ◆ Nearby airport, industrial centers, or retail and commercial congestion
- ◆ Poor school system reputation
- ◆ Business and industry moving out of the area
- ◆ Higher-than-average crime rates
- ◆ Sellers offering a number of concessions to try to attract buyers

With a little investigation and some input from your real estate agent, you can quickly determine the best neighborhoods in your area. Once you have a feel for it, unless a major event occurs, you don't have to worry that a "good" neighborhood will suddenly become a "bad" neighborhood. Changes take place over time. For example, over the past 15 to 20 years, the "Fan" district of Richmond, VA has undergone a major renewal as homeowners have improved rundown and poorly maintained properties. Long an area that discriminating buyers avoided, this area has become popular with young professionals, and prices have skyrocketed. But it took a number of years for the area to gain momentum.

Take the time to learn the ins and outs of your area: Location, location, location are still the three most important factors in valuing real estate. A great house in a lousy neighborhood will never reach its full value potential.

 Look for "don't-wanners"—homes the owners want to get rid of so badly that they are willing to accept anything. Ideally, you want a don't-wanner home in a *do-wanner neighborhood*—a diamond in the rough amid a block of shiny diamonds. Although we focus on foreclosures in this book, you can often find great deals on properties simply by driving around good neighborhoods, finding don't-wanners, and then talking with the neighbors to get in contact with the homeowners. Don't-wanners stand out. They often have overgrown landscapes, newspapers piled up on the porch, and an empty look to them.

MYTH # **39**

I Shouldn't Bring in Experts to Help Me Analyze the Deal; the Fewer People Who Know It's Available, the Better.

Fact: You Need the Experts, So Deal Only with People You Trust

First let's dispel a different myth: There are no "secret" deals. If you have found a foreclosure opportunity, others can find it too—foreclosures are public knowledge. So spending your time being secretive and playing cloak-and-dagger games is a waste of effort.

At the same time, information is valuable, and information you have developed is very valuable, if to no one else but you. Developing that information takes time and often requires bringing in expert help. So, while you don't want to give away your hard-earned knowledge, at the same time it pays to get the expert advice.

Sound like a tough balance to strike? It's not. Here's a simple rule of thumb we follow: Always deal only with people you trust. (Why would you ever deal with someone you *don't* trust?) If, for example, a contractor you asked for advice about the potential repair costs for a particular property ends up next to you on the courthouse steps bidding against you for that property at the foreclosure auction, never deal with him or her again. (And don't get mad and bid higher than your walk-away price just to make sure he or she doesn't end up with the property. If you're that angry, walk away and let the deal go.)

If a member of your expert team seems really interested in an opportunity, consider going partners on the deal. You'll spread your risk, leverage your skills, and develop an even closer working relationship with that person, which *builds trust* and a stronger team.

When you are first starting out, become an information sponge. Soak up everything that everyone with more experience has to tell you. This doesn't mean you necessarily have to act on that information or follow other people's recommendations. Just gather the information. You can sort it out later, put some of it to good use, and ignore the recommendations you don't value. More people than you realize will share information with you, as long as you invest with integrity, show a sincere interest in learning, and demonstrate a passion for investing. You need to be willing to share, too.

SECTION 5

Financing the Property

F inding and analyzing foreclosure properties are only the first steps. Now you have to nail down the deal and find the money! From government loans to private money and home equity loans—there's enough willing people *and* enough money to go around when the deal is good! Here we look at some of the most common myths about getting a foreclosure property financed.

MYTH # **40**

Interest on Loans from Private Investors Is Too High.

Fact: Access to Money Is Often More Important than the Cost of Borrowing It

Say you check out a foreclosure property thoroughly, and the more you see, the more excited you become. The neighborhood is great; the house is in excellent shape; you see no barriers to getting good title; and the home-owners have significant equity in the property. Based on your knowledge of property values and the prices foreclosure properties tend to bring, you feel sure you can make $50,000 to $70,000 on the deal. It's a home run!

But there's a problem. Where you live you need a 10% deposit at time of auction and the remainder of the purchase price within 48 hours. You can't get a loan that quickly from a bank; what will you do?

You can use your home, your possessions, your credit cards, and even your retirement fund as collateral on the loan, but there is another option: *hard money*.

Hard money is a high-interest, short-term loan, and you can often find hard money loans through your mortgage broker or from investors in your area. Sometimes you will find them listed in the newspaper or business magazines. These investors include private finance groups (such as doctors or attorneys), local mortgage bankers, insurance funds, pension funds, REITs, or just regular folks looking for a good place to park their money. Hard money offers three major benefits:

1. Hard money lenders often accept the future value of the property as collateral; that way you don't have to borrow against your home or other assets, and you might be able to borrow enough to cover the purchase price and the cost of rehabbing the home.
2. You can set up a separate escrow account with a hard money lender to fund repairs and renovations.
3. You get access to financing you may not be able to get through a conventional lender.

The flip side is that hard money loans naturally cost more; that's why they call it *hard* money. Investors incur risk making the loan, and they want a return for that risk. You can expect the following:

◆ **Points:** Hard money lenders often require you to pay between two and six points (or more) up front. One point is 1% of the loan value. For a $100,000 loan at four points you'll pay $4,000 just for the privilege of getting the loan.
◆ **Interest:** Interest rates are naturally higher, sometimes double the going rate for conventional loans. If the current rate for a fixed-rate mortgage is 7%, you can expect to pay between 12 and 14% for a hard money loan.

- **Loan-to-value:** Loan-to-value (LTV) is the ratio of the loan to the value of the property. A loan of $100,000 on a property valued at $100,000 has an LTV rate of 100%. Hard money lenders will typically loan only 50% to at most 70% of the expected sale price of the property (not the purchase price; the eventual sale price). Depending on what you pay for the property, you may need additional funds to cover repairs or holding costs.
- **Amortization:** The term of the loan will be typically between 3 and 15 years, rather than 20 or 30; the hard money lender wants you to pay the principal down more quickly. As a result, your monthly payments will be higher. Your lender will sometimes reduce the fees or points if the loan is paid off faster!
- **Balloon payment:** Many hard money loans have balloon payments; instead of making equal payments over the life of the loan, the final payment is the remaining balance. If you amortize the loan over 10 years but have a balloon payment at the end of two years, the sum can be considerable. Some hard money lenders may require that the loan be paid in full after 12 or even 6 months. If you line up other financing in the meantime or flip the house, that's not a problem; if you don't, you'll need to have sufficient funds on hand.
- **Prepayment penalties:** Some hard money lenders want a predictable flow of income and stipulate a prepayment penalty if you pay the loan off early, so know your terms.
- **Closing costs:** Hard money loans are closed like conventional loans. You can be required to pay any fee or points you agree to up front, so make sure you fully understand your responsibilities at closing before you agree to the loan.

Does this sound scary? It can be, but only if you don't take the time to understand the deal and what that means to your investment. The profit the hard money investor makes is irrelevant; what matters is *your* profit. Simply factor the cost of financing into your calculations, just as you would repair costs or real estate commissions or any other cost. If you can make a return you are happy with, does it matter how much the hard money lender makes on the deal? Chip once put together a deal where the investor charged 12 points at 15% interest! It didn't matter, as it was short-term money, and the profit was still over $270,000! Don't let the numbers or the cost of the hard money loan blind you to the profits involved in the deal.

If working with a hard money lender costs you, say, an additional $8,000, but that's the only way you can make the deal, and you'll still make $30,000 in profit, the hard money lender may be a great option after all.

A $30,000 profit you can make is infinitely better than a $38,000 profit you have no way of making.

(STOP) Don't overlook holding costs. If you have only enough money to cover the purchase price and repairs and renovations, the unexpected holding costs could derail your investment and possibly lead to your losing the home in foreclosure. Include all costs in your calculations and make sure you have sufficient funds on hand plus at least a 10% buffer to cover the unexpected.

MYTH # **41**

Lenders Don't Want to Deal with Little Ole Me.

Fact: Lenders Need You, Because If They Don't Make Loans They Don't Make Money

A lender without borrowers is a lender that is out of business.

Lenders need you. They make money by lending to people like you. A lender isn't doing you a favor by approving your loan; instead they are generating revenue through application fees, points, and the interest charged on your loan. Without you, the lender doesn't exist.

While it is true that mortgage lenders like to make large loans to major clients, their bread and butter is actually homeowners and small investors like you. By working with hundreds and thousands of clients they spread their risk and diversify their loan portfolios.

And, investors, like little 'ole you, are a great source of repeat business. A mortgage broker would love to make 2, 3, 10, or more loans to you each year. Let your mortgage broker know you plan to invest in real estate and you're looking for a lending partner; if he or she doesn't seem interested, look elsewhere. Believe us, dozens of mortgage brokers in your area would *love* to do business with you.

You can make yourself a more attractive borrower. Work on increasing your net worth (the total value of what you own minus what you owe). Check your credit report regularly and correct any discrepancies. Pay your bills on time. Try to save some money. The more attractive you are as a borrower, the more money you can borrow and the less you have to pay to borrow it. Borrowers who represent a high level of risk pay dearly for it.

MYTH # **42**

Lenders Won't Be Willing to Talk to Me Until I Have a Deal on the Table.

Fact: Good Lenders Will Talk to You Well Ahead of Time

Successfully investing in foreclosure properties, whether during pre-foreclosure, at auction, or even at the REO stage, often requires you to act fast. Access to financing is critical.

A good lender will help you get prepared to act quickly by evaluating your financial means, giving you advice, assessing your potential investment opportunities, and preapproving you for financing.

Note that *preapproval* differs greatly from *prequalification*:

Prequalified simply means you have described your financial situation to a lender, and the lender has given an opinion about whether you will possibly qualify for a loan. Prequalification is simply the lender's opinion based on information received; prequalification does not indicate that the lender has reviewed your credit report or verified any of the information you provided.

Think of it this way: A prequalification letter basically says, "I, the lender, feel that this individual is *probably* qualified for a loan of this size *if* everything he or she told me regarding his or her financial situation is accurate." Not exactly a ringing endorsement, would you say?

Preapproved means you have provided documentation proving your income, assets, liabilities, and other factors the lender needs to evaluate your financial solvency. The lender has checked your credit report, and most of the paperwork needed for your loan probably has been prepared.

A preapproval letter basically says, "I, the lender, have reviewed all necessary documentation and have run appropriate credit checks to ensure that this individual *will* qualify for a loan of this size." All you're really waiting for at this point is a property appraisal and title!

If you've been preapproved for a loan of, say, $200,000, then you can act much more quickly on a deal because, in essence, the lender will need only to assess the value of the property you intend to purchase to make sure the collateral value of the property is sufficient and check the title to ensure everything is in order.

A good lender will also take the time to give you advice on how to improve your credit rating, improve your net worth, and gather up the documentation you need to satisfy underwriting requirements, and will even give you a sense of which types of real estate investments make sense for you based on your financial situation and your goals. While it will cost the lender time, good lenders see time spent working with you as an investment that will pay off as your real estate investing career takes off. Lenders want to establish a solid business relationship with successful investors, just as you want to establish a solid business relationship with a good lender.

Once you have a solid track record showing that you have bought and sold foreclosure properties for a profit in the past, lenders will be more willing to work with you. When you are first starting out, and you have no track record, it helps for you to show the lender that you know what you're doing. Find a foreclosure property in your area and write up a plan showing the maximum you would pay for that property, estimates of how much it would cost to fix up, how long it would require to sell, and your estimated profit. This shows the lender that you are able to plan ahead, even if you don't end up buying this particular property.

MYTH # **43**

I Should Use as Much of My *Own* Money as Possible.

Fact: You Take on Less Risk and Maximize Your Profit Potential by Using as Much of Other People's Money as Possible

Novice investors are often reluctant to borrow money. They don't want to risk losing someone else's money and having that person become upset with them. As a result, they may make some terrible decisions, such as cashing out all of the equity in their own homes, cashing out their retirement accounts, or using their businesses as collateral for loans. This approach unnecessarily exposes their personal assets to risk and may even compromise potential tax savings (if they cash out retirement accounts, for example).

In addition, by using all of their own money, they gain no leverage. Wealth is created through leverage. The limited amount of money they have access to limits the type of home they can afford to buy, thus limiting the maximum amount of profit.

As an investor, you should try to use as much of other people's money (OPM) as possible. By borrowing from hard money lenders, you will pay more for the money you borrow; but you may be able to convince the lender to finance the entire investment (purchase price, repair and renovation expenses, and holding costs), assuming the lender is willing to accept the future value of the property as collateral for the loan.

Another way to obtain a good chunk of the financing you need is to convince a bank to put up the money in one of the following ways:

♦ Instead of obtaining your own financing to purchase the home in pre-foreclosure, ask the distressed homeowners' lender if the lender would allow you to assume the homeowners' current mortgage loan.

In such a case, you would simply take over the homeowner's monthly payments until you could rehab and sell the home and pay off the balance of the mortgage.

- If you buy REO properties from banks, the bank may be willing to finance the purchase of the property, simply to divest itself of the property and get the bad loan off of its books. Chip has purchased many properties this way, often with no down-payment requirement!

You can always use your own money, of course, but as an investor, you should do everything possible to cover your assets while seeking to extend your lead. We don't want to see you in foreclosure.

Another way to protect your personal assets is to create your own LLC (limited liability corporation) for buying and selling foreclosures. By operating as an LLC, you protect yourself against any lawsuits that homeowners, contractors, or other parties may file against you for whatever reason. Consult your attorney to discuss the benefits and drawbacks of LLCs and to set up your LLC for you, should you decide that it is a good idea.

MYTH # **44**

I Can't Use FHA or VA Financing.

Fact: A Property Is a Property; You and the Property Simply Have to Qualify under FHA or VA Guidelines

You can secure government-backed financing to purchase a foreclosure property, but keep the following restrictions in mind:

- FHA and VA financing require you to live in the home; you can't use government-backed loans to finance homes you intend to purchase as investment properties.
- As with conventional loans, the process for obtaining approval for an FHA or VA loan can take some time. If you're purchasing the house

at auction and the total sales price is due within days or even weeks, you may need to get a hard-money loan to bridge the gap until you can close on the FHA or VA loan.

As we noted earlier, if you purchase a home that was repossessed by the VA, you do not need to be a veteran of the military, but you will still have to sign a statement showing your intent to live in the house.

Some investors simply lie about their intent to live in the home in order to obtain FHA or VA financing. We strongly discourage you from doing the same. In addition to losing your financing and the home, if the lender finds out about it, you can also expect to pay a hefty fine and perhaps even do some jail time. Lying on a loan application is a felony.

MYTH # **45**

I Can't Use a Home Equity Loan to Finance the Property, Since I Don't Own the Property Yet.

Fact: Home Equity Loan Funds Can Be Used for Any Purpose, Including to Buy a Foreclosure Property

As we explained in our previous book, *Mortgage Myths*, if you've paid down your mortgage, or if your home's value has risen in the past few years, you could have significant equity you can pull out of your home. *Equity* refers to the difference between your home's value and the outstanding balance on your mortgage. If your home is worth $400,000 and you only owe $200,000 on it, you have $200,000 in equity in the home.

You can use that equity to finance the purchase of a foreclosure property, either in whole or in part, depending on the price of the foreclosure property. At the very least, you may decide to use home equity funds to pay the deposit at the foreclosure auction or for repair and renovation costs once you own the property.

If you have decided you want to remove some amount of equity from your home, there are two main ways to do so:

- **Refinance your original mortgage.** Say you own a $300,000 home and you owe only $100,000 on your mortgage; you could refinance that loan, borrowing $200,000, using $100,000 to pay off the balance on your original mortgage and the other $100,000 to invest in foreclosures (and keeping about $100,000 equity in your home as a safety net). Many people choose this option, but there are at least two main disadvantages: You'll pay closing costs on the new loan and you'll start making interest payments on the higher loan balance immediately and for the life of the new loan.
- **Take out a home equity loan.** A home equity loan doesn't affect your first mortgage and doesn't require an extensive documentation or approval process because the risk to the lender is typically covered by the value of your home.

There are two subtypes of home equity loans: A *home equity loan* and a *home equity line of credit*. The main difference is that proceeds from a home equity loan are distributed immediately; if you take out a $50,000 home equity *loan*, you get those funds immediately and you start making payments on the full amount immediately. A home equity line is a *line of credit* up to a maximum amount. If you take out a $50,000 home equity *line*, that amount is available to you, but you don't have to draw all (or any) of it out at any given time; you use it when you need it or want it. If you need only $10,000 today, great; draw that $10,000 and you'll make payments only on that $10,000, not on the entire $50,000 as you would if you got a home equity loan.

As a result, a home equity line is almost always the better choice, because even if you'll eventually need to use the entire available line of credit, you can delay your spending appropriately to avoid unnecessary interest payments. Plus, as you pay down your home equity line, you can withdraw from the available balance as many times as you like.

Home equity lines are harder to get when the market contracts (during times of tight credit), but if you are a strong borrower with lots of equity, it should still be a viable option. Another option is the use of credit cards.

Don't do this unless you know what you're doing, or you could end up in trouble! But, we have financed a ton of properties (and repairs) through the use of unsecured credit card lines.

 Even if you don't need a home equity line of credit to invest in real estate, we strongly recommend that you apply for a home equity line of credit. A line of credit gives you a buffer in the event that cash flow becomes a problem. You can draw from your account at any time and then simply pay the money back when you get it. Sure, you'll pay some interest on the money you draw out, but if you pay it back quickly, the interest is usually pretty minimal and is tax-deductible mortgage interest.

MYTH # **46**

Since the Property Is Already in Foreclosure, I Can't Assume the Owner's Loan.

Fact: The Lender May Want You to Assume the Loan

As we mentioned earlier, lenders don't want to foreclose. They want to make loans, collect fees, and collect payments. They have no desire to incur the time and expense required to foreclose and then sell the property. Lenders don't make money on foreclosures; in fact, they often *lose* money.

And remember, a homeowner in the foreclosure process has not yet been foreclosed on. He can bring payments current, make other arrangements with the lender, or even sell the house—up to the date of the foreclosure auction, at least.

Assuming a loan simply means that you take over the owner's mortgage. You then become officially responsible for repaying the loan. In effect you "buy" the house by taking over the mortgage.

Why would you assume a loan? Because you might get a lower interest rate than is currently available, have an easier time qualifying for the loan, put little or no money down, and you'll definitely pay lower closing costs.

Years ago, nearly all mortgages were assumable. Starting in the late 1970s, most lenders began inserting a "due-on-sale" clause into their mortgages to prohibit assumptions. Many people now believe that all loans are nonassumable, but that's not the case.

In general, almost all FHA, VA, and adjustable rate mortgages (ARMs) offer assumption privileges to buyers. Some conventional loans and sub-prime mortgages will also allow assumptions. To find out whether a particular homeowner's mortgage loan is assumable, all you have to do is ask or inspect the mortgage contract (the Note).

If the loan is a non-FHA or -VA loan, the mortgage most likely includes language like the following:

> If all or any part of the mortgaged property or an interest therein is sold or transferred by the borrower without the lender's prior written consent, the lender may, at the lender's option, declare all the sums secured by the mortgage to be immediately due and payable.

If the homeowner's mortgage contains wording such as this and he sells or in any way transfers ownership of the property, the lender has the right to expect immediate repayment of the full loan balance if it hasn't given you (the investor) prior written consent to assume the mortgage.

Ask most "experts" if they think a loan is assumable and they'll say, "No, because of the due-on-sale clause." That may not be the case, though; the loan is still assumable if the owner gets written consent from the lender.

Why would a lender give its consent? For any or all of the following reasons:

- The owner has fallen behind on payments, you will bring the mortgage current, and the lender won't have to foreclose and face the hassle and expense of preparing the home, listing it, and selling it.
- You already do business with the lender, and you have established a good business relationship.
- The interest rate on the mortgage is higher than the current market rate, so the lender will protect the return on its money.

The last point may surprise you. Why should you assume a mortgage with a higher rate than you can get from another lender?

While it may cost you a little more, if you plan to flip the house, the difference in higher payments may cost you less than the closing costs you'll incur if you get another mortgage. Plus, if you're in the process of assuming the loan, the lender may put off the foreclosure auction until the transaction is finalized.

Never assume anything—except a mortgage if it's in your best interest! Ask questions. Ask for help. Ask if you can assume a nonassumable loan. You just might be able to.

Just because you can assume the owner's mortgage, that doesn't necessarily mean you would want to. If the home has several other liens against it and you assume the first mortgage, you may take on the responsibility of paying off those other loans, too. In such a case, you would probably be better off buying the property at the foreclosure auction, so the foreclosure would wipe out any junior liens. Check the title and county records!

MYTH # **47**

The Property Has to Be in Good Shape to Get Financing.

Fact: Lenders Finance Properties in Poor Shape Every Day

First let's look at how lenders decide whether to approve a loan.

From a lender's point of view, a "good loan" is a loan made to a borrower who demonstrates both the *ability* and the *willingness* to repay that loan. Your current financial situation determines your *ability* to repay. Your *willingness* to repay is determined largely by your past credit history and thus your credit score—in other words, how you've handled credit in the past.

Lenders ask two basic questions about your ability to pay. First, is your income large enough to cover the expenses associated with the loan plus any existing debt obligations that will continue in the future? Second, do you have enough cash to meet the up-front cash requirements of the loan? (In other words, can you cover the down payment, closing costs, and monthly payments?)

Other factors come into play; one of the main variables evaluated is the property's loan-to-value ratio (LTV). The loan-to-value ratio is the percentage relationship between the amount borrowed and the appraised value or sale price of the property, typically whichever is lower.

For example, if you buy a house for $200,000, and you borrow $160,000, then the LTV is 80%: $160,000 divided by $200,000. (The more you put down, the lower the LTV.)

Why is the LTV ratio important? The lower the LTV, the less risk the lender faces, and the more likely the lender is to approve your loan. If your credit is poor, the lender may require a lower LTV than for an individual with good credit.

Because the lender evaluates your ability to repay, your willingness to repay, and the LTV ratio, among other factors, a property in poor condition stands as good a chance for loan approval as a property in outstanding condition, as long as the LTV ratio meets the lender's guidelines.

Say a particular property, if well maintained and in good condition, would have a fair market value of $200,000. It's in poor shape, however, and its value is closer to $150,000. You won't qualify for an $180,000 loan from a conventional lender; the LTV ratio is extremely unfavorable. If you can buy the property for $100,000 and finance the entire purchase price, the LTV ratio is 66%—and the lender may happily approve the loan.

There are other programs available, too, such as an FHA 203(k) loan that can lend on future value. While this program is not open to investors (unless HUD owns the property), this is a great way to get into your own home and have the government finance (and insure) the rehabilitation!

Loan approval is like a jigsaw puzzle; all the pieces must fit. A poorly maintained piece may fit perfectly with the rest of the pieces of your puzzle.

 If you're turned down for a particular loan, don't assume that being turned down is a bad thing. Think of it as getting a second opinion. Perhaps the lender thinks that the chance of making a profit off the property is not all that great and has saved you from making a costly mistake. Take the rejection in stride and keep looking for better investment opportunities.

MYTH # **48**

Taking on a Partner Will Merely Cut into My Profits.

Fact: While You May Reduce Your Profits, You'll Reduce Your Overall Risk and Leverage Your Combined Efforts and Expertise

Partners share responsibilities, risk, and profits. Many people avoid partnerships because they don't want to share profits, but that's a short-sighted view. (And we practice what we preach; we wrote this book as partners because we each bring unique strengths and experience to the table. We have also gone into partnerships with people on lots of different properties!) A good partner can help keep you motivated and on track, and keep you from feeling like you're on your own when times get tough.

There's another reason to take on a partner: if you can't buy the property any other way. Your partner may bring cash or financing you can't manage. Or your partner may have the skills to help make repairs and renovations that you otherwise couldn't afford to make without cutting deeply into your potential profits.

Here's a simple way to look at it: Say you have a source for hard money financing but you still need $10,000 in cash to make repairs and renovations. Finding a partner with ready cash makes all the difference; you may share your profits, but that's better than letting the deal go and making no money.

Chip remembers one of his early foreclosure deals. He had all sorts of time, energy, and know-how to rehab and fix up the property, but not much cash. A Realtor® he knew came in and provided the funds, and six months later they split the profits! A true win-win for both partners.

When two or more persons go into business together, they usually form some sort of formal partnership. It's fairly easy to set up a partnership and doesn't cost much in the way of attorney's fees.

Among the advantages of partnership is the division of equipment, supplies, or labor. On the flipside, a division of responsibilities can lead to disagreements. If you're considering a partnership, you'll have to answer some basic questions:

- ◆ Will you carry equal workloads? If not, how will you divide work responsibilities?
- ◆ Will investments be made equally?
- ◆ Will profits be shared equally?
- ◆ Who has the final say in case there is a disagreement?

If you decide to take on a partner, make sure you create a comprehensive written agreement. The more complete your agreement, the fewer the disagreements you'll have down the line. Spend time considering, discussing, and writing down everything pertaining to your partnership. Put everything in writing. Don't go into the partnership assuming you'll be able to work out any problems if they come up. When things get sticky, you probably won't be willing or able to resolve your differences.

After you've written up your agreement, give an attorney a copy of the document. The attorney should draft an agreement for approval by all parties. After corrections, additions, and deletions, the attorney will draft the final agreement for you and your partners' signatures.

The agreement should make provisions for division of expenditures, profits, losses, responsibilities, and liabilities as well as long-term illness, disability, or death of a partner.

No matter how well you think you'll get along, assume in your partnership agreement that the worst might happen and plan accordingly for what will take place. If your prospective partner objects to putting together a detailed agreement, find another partner.

STOP Your partnership agreement should also function as a prenuptial agreement; that is, how will you divide any partner-owned assets should you and your partners decide to split up? When forming a partnership, everyone involved usually has stars in their eyes as they dream about their ideal future together. When significant problems arise and end the partnership, they have no exit strategy and are now so upset with one another that they cannot resolve a fair and equitable breakup. Have an exit strategy in place from day one.

SECTION 6

Securing the Property

How do you actually take physical possession of the property? What about the former owners or "squatters" who could be occupying your new investment? In this section, we look at some of the more serious myths surrounding the security and protection of your interest in the property.

MYTH # **49**

Once I Purchase the Property at Auction, I Can Take Immediate Possession.

Fact: The Previous Owners May Be Able to Redeem the Property after Reimbursing You for the Purchase Price, Interest, and Qualifying Expenses

Some areas have what is called a mandatory *redemption period*. During the redemption period, the homeowners have the legal right to redeem the property, but only if they reimburse the person who purchased the home at auction the full purchase price along with any interest, taxes, and other qualifying expenses the investor paid and filed an affidavit for having paid.

During this time, you, the "owner" of the property, must pay the property taxes and insurance. Depending on local guidelines for redemption, you may have the right to recover expenses from the homeowner if the person ultimately redeems the property; see your real estate attorney for the specifics for your area.

You will frequently end up with the property regardless of a redemption period. In order to redeem the property, the homeowners will have to experience a *major* change in their financial situation, or be rescued by a wealthy friend or relative. The odds are fairly low of this happening (although occasionally it does), so while you're waiting, take the following steps to protect your investment until the redemption period expires:

- **Insure the property.** If the property is damaged or destroyed during the redemption period, and you don't have an insurance policy on it, you could lose your entire investment (this has happened more often than you might think). Rates for insuring an investment property are typically higher than rates for a typical homeowner's policy because the insurance company's risk is higher: Owner-occupants tend to take better care of a property than a renter or an "ex-owner" remaining in the house during the redemption period.

- **Pay property taxes.** If you fail to make property tax payments, the tax collector can foreclose on the property and sell a tax deed or lien to collect the money owed. If another investor buys the tax deed or lien, you could lose your investment. As the new owner, you are responsible for paying the property taxes.

- **Keep an eye on the property.** Try to protect it from vandalism or theft. Some homeowners may damage the property or try to remove items that should remain before they leave, like cabinets, outbuildings, and so on. If you notice anything suspicious, call the police.

- **Make necessary repairs.** *Necessary* repairs are repairs to defects that make the house unsafe or could lead to further damage or deterioration. Fixing a leaky roof is a necessary repair; repainting the house because you hate the color is not.

- **Don't make unnecessary renovations.** Remember, the homeowners may redeem the property, and you could lose your investment in renovations. (You may not even have the option of making repairs, since abandonment laws in some states may restrict you from doing anything to the property.) Make necessary repairs, not renovations or improvements. Save your improvements until after the redemption period, when the property is definitely yours.

Make sure you file affidavits proving that you paid the property taxes and insurance premiums (and any other qualifying expenses) the day you make those payments. If you wait, the house may be redeemed in the interim and you'll definitely lose the right to be reimbursed for those expenses.

You may wish to take some of the uncertainty out of the redemption period by securing a *nonredemption certificate*. A nonredemption certificate is not a deed; it's an agreement between you and the homeowners that they will not seek to redeem the property. You'll likely need to offer some compensation to receive the certificate—we like to call this "cash for keys." In effect, you offer the homeowners, for example, $2,000 if they will give you the keys and a signed nonredemption certificate. (If you can, structure the agreement so they receive a portion of the agreed-upon amount up front and the remainder when the redemption period has officially expired. Splitting the payments can help motivate them to stick with the agreement and keep them from trying to move back in prior to the expiration of the redemption period.)

Talk to your attorney before you contact homeowners about nonredemption. In some areas, asking homeowners to relinquish their rights can be considered unethical, and the agreement difficult to enforce. The last thing you want is for it to appear that you tried to take advantage of homeowners in distress, so try to have no contact with the homeowners during the last month of the redemption period. Be proactive and try to make any agreements or arrangements early in the redemption period rather than near the end.

 In areas that have a mandatory redemption period, that period may be shortened considerably if the homeowners abandon the property, leaving the home vacant. The courts are well aware that vacant homes tend to attract criminals and other riffraff, so they speed up the process. Consult your real estate attorney to determine the rules that govern vacant properties in redemption. Under no circumstances should you try to coerce the homeowner into abandoning the property early by misleading them about their rights; for example, some disreputable investors may tell the homeowner that they purchased the property at auction and the homeowner must immediately vacate the premises when, in fact, the homeowner has the right to stay in the home for several months.

MYTH # **50**

Only Real Estate Pros Are Allowed to Attend Real Estate Auctions.

Fact: Foreclosure Auctions Are by Law Public Auctions

Foreclosure auctions aren't terribly exciting, except for the people actually bidding, so while it's true that usually only real estate pros do attend, anyone has the legal right to attend. And you don't have to do anything to exercise that legal right—simply show up at the right place at the right time. (The time, location, and other details of the auction are listed in the foreclosure notices printed in your paper or available at the courthouse.) No one will try to stop you from attending, and no one will ask you for proof that you have a right to be there. In fact, no one will probably even notice you unless you draw attention to yourself.

Go to as many foreclosure auctions as you can, even if you're not interested in the property. Each time you'll get a better feel for the process and for the regulars who usually attend.

Over time, you'll also develop a sense of price. A property in foreclosure will almost always sell for less than it would if it were sold on the open market. Checking out properties for sale and then attending the auctions will help you develop the ability to calculate foreclosure values from an insider's point of view. And it's a free education, because the process and auctions are open to the public.

So, what are you waiting for? Attend some auctions!

Although anyone can attend a foreclosure auction, many auctions do not allow just anyone to bid. Many jurisdictions that have had trouble with bidders not following through on their purchases have enacted rules that prevent the ill-prepared from placing bids. You may need to show up with a certified check that covers either the opening bid amount or at least a 10% deposit, or get *preapproved* as a bidder in advance. Make sure you know the rules before you show up to bid.

MYTH # **51**

There Will Be Lots of People Bidding against Me.

Fact: In Most Towns, Very Few People Attend the Auction—Sometimes Only the Lender's Representative

In the previous myth, we urged you to attend auctions. What we didn't tell you is that the average auction can be, well, less than exciting. Sometimes the only person attending, other than the attorney conducting the sale, is the lender's representative. Most of the time, a few other people will attend, but only one might actually bid. The first bid will usually be made by a representative of the foreclosing lender. The lender can bid up the amount owed. If no one else bids, the lender gets the property and it becomes an REO property.

That's why in many cases no one shows up but the auctioneer and the lender's representative. The less equity the homeowners have in the property, the less likely it is that the property will be attractive to investors, and the less likely that many people will show up.

Even if the property does have investment potential, relatively few people will attend. After attending a few auctions, you'll come to recognize the regulars in your area; most are investors like you, but a few, such as people who frequently attend public hearings, may attend just for the free entertainment.

You'll also get a sense for how each regular likes to bid. Some only want properties if they can win at rock-bottom prices; they'll quickly stop bidding once the price reaches a reasonable level. Others won't bid until all the casual bidders have been shaken out; they try to hide their interest in the property until the last minute. Don't be fooled by this behavior; if they weren't interested in the property, they wouldn't attend the auction in the first place. (Still others will bid *once* early on, just for the sheer thrill of having placed a bid.)

While you will learn to spot the regulars, remember that in the end it doesn't matter how many people attend the auction. A good investment is a good investment, and a bad investment is a bad investment. We've purchased great foreclosure properties when, aside from the lender's rep and the auctioneer, we were the only other people in attendance. We've also attended packed auctions for properties where the lender's initial bid was higher than the value of the home. How many people attend is unimportant; all that matters is whether you can get the property at a price your analysis indicates will give you an excellent chance of making a profit.

The number of investors who show up to bid on properties can also be influenced by the number of properties being sold at auction. Just be sure that if you show up to bid, you show up prepared. Have a folder for each property you're interested in bidding on and a certified check for the amount necessary to secure the property should you win the bid. Before the bidding starts on a property, review your notes and recommit yourself to not bidding above your walk-away price.

MYTH # **52**

The Higher the Bidding Goes, and the More People Bidding, the More Likely It's a Great Property.

Fact: Many Bidders Give in to Their Emotions, and Bidding Spirals out of Control Simply Because People Don't Like to Lose

Investors come from all walks of life and backgrounds. Some investors, like you, will approach the process rationally and objectively, seeking to minimize or control risk while maximizing their return. Others will try to be rational but occasionally fail, especially at an auction.

Auctions are competitions. One party wins the auction, and the others lose. ("Winning" is sometimes subjective; we've lost properties at auction to other bidders only to later realize we were glad we weren't the high bidder.) The competitive nature of an auction leads to a variety of emotions: Attend auctions, and on the faces of bidders you may see fear, anxiety, excitement, apprehension, and even panic or anger when a bidder feels a property is slipping away.

Some properties are great investment opportunities, and a number of people will bid. The more people there are who are interested, the higher the bidding will go. Some properties are poor investments, and a number of people will bid.

Why is this so? It's called *buyer's panic.* Buyer's panic occurs when a bidder thinks this property is the investment of a lifetime, and he'll never get another chance at such an amazing opportunity. When he sees the property slipping away, buyer's panic sets in, and he bids too high. Others may also fall under the spell of buyer's panic, or may simply think, "Wow, he's bidding higher and higher. . . . He must know something I don't know. . . . I *can't* let this property slip away!" Buyer's panic typically breeds further competition between bidders and causes the price to spiral further out of control.

The supply of foreclosure properties is vast. You are under no pressure whatsoever to buy any particular property, no matter how much time and effort you've put into investigating the deal. If you're interested in the property and have done your homework, you've developed your maximum or walk-away bid amount. (If you haven't done your homework, you should *never* bid.) Employ any bid strategy you like at the auction (we covered a few in Myth #37) and, no matter how many people bid, *never* bid higher than *your* maximum bid amount.

Any time the bidding goes past your walk-away price, stop bidding and take the time to watch the play of emotions on the other bidders' faces. You'll be surprised what you can learn about the subjective and emotional aspect of auctions—especially about what *not* to do.

Remember, the higher the bid, the lower the profit potential and the higher the risk. You make your profit when you buy a property. If you pay too much, thinking you will make up the difference when you sell, you are making a costly mistake. Buy for the right price, and you have a much better chance of earning a profit when it comes time to sell.

MYTH # **53**

I Won't Be Able to Get Good Title to the Property.

Fact: Mechanics Liens and Back Taxes Don't Go Away, but You Learn All About the Title at the Courthouse Ahead of Time

The title is the most important document attached to a property. The title lists the legal owners of the property along with any lien holders or claims against the property. For example, if you purchased your home using a mortgage, the mortgage company's name appears on the title as a lien holder.

You absolutely must look at the title before you try to purchase a house from the homeowners or at auction. If you don't:

- ◆ You may buy a junior lien thinking you are buying the senior lien. Once foreclosure runs its course, your junior lien may be wiped out, leaving you with nothing.
- ◆ You could end up purchasing the home from the homeowners after another investor has already bought the senior lien, creating a legal mess that could be costly to sort out and make it difficult or impossible to get all of your money back. Under duress, some homeowners may attempt to defraud investors using strategies like this. (If you buy directly from homeowners, make sure you purchase title insurance and have your title company handle the closing to help you avoid nasty and costly surprises.)

- You could end up purchasing a property another buyer has recently closed on. A con artist may sell the same home to several different buyers. While this situation is relatively rare, it can and does happen.

Here's what you should look for on the title:

- Homeowner's names: Make sure the mortgagor's name matches the name listed as the actual property title holder.
- Date purchased and price paid: You can get a sense of the property's current value by knowing when it was purchased and how much was paid. This will give you a better feel for what the homeowners will hope to get when they sell.
- Deed names: The names on the deed should match the names on the title.
- Previous mortgagor: Examine the *chain of title* (the past several titles issued for the property) and look for any gaps in ownership. If Person A sold the property to Person B and then Person C sold to Person D, to whom did Person B sell the house? Something's missing, which could indicate a problem in the chain of ownership, which could keep you from getting clear title.
- Current first mortgage holder: The first mortgage holder holds the senior lien on the property.
- Second mortgage holder(s): Second mortgage holders hold the junior liens on the property.
- IRS federal income tax liens.
- State income tax liens.
- Property tax liens.
- Other liens: Mechanics liens or construction liens.

Your title company can also perform a title search for you, and so can your lawyer. We recommend you learn to research titles yourself; you'll save time and money, and you'll gain more experience with real estate transactions. If you find things you don't understand, then you can consult your title company or attorney for advice and clarification.

Now let's talk about title insurance. Title insurance protects against loss arising from problems connected to the title to your property. Before you purchased a foreclosure property, it probably went through several ownership changes, and the land on which it stands may have gone through many more. A weak link at any point in that chain of ownership could cause trouble. For example, someone along the way may have forged a signature in transferring title, or there may be unpaid real estate taxes or other liens against the property.

Title insurance covers the insured party for any claims and legal fees that arise out of such problems, protecting against losses from events that occurred prior to the date of the policy. In other words, the coverage period ends on the day the policy is issued and extends backward in time for an indefinite period. (Title insurance works the opposite way life insurance does; life insurance protects against losses resulting from events that occur *after* the policy is issued for a specified time period extending into the *future*.)

For example, if the contractor you failed to pay for building an addition places a lien on the property, you are not protected by your title policy because the lien was placed after the date of issue.

Title insurance protects against losses that might occur due to another party claiming ownership of the property.

Title insurance covers:

◆ Issues missed by the title examiner
◆ Issues missed when a deed or other public document is determined to be invalid or forged
◆ Liens from unpaid taxes or from a former owner

Title insurance will pay your legal fees if you have to go to court to defend the deed, and if you lose the property, the title insurance will cover your loss up to the amount of the policy.

Keep in mind that if you've owned the property for a few years and it has risen in value, the title insurance policy you purchased at closing will merely reimburse you for the original amount, not for the new value of the property.

You may be thinking, "Wait a minute. . . . If I pay an attorney to perform a title search, why do I need title insurance? Isn't it the attorney's job to make sure the title is clear?" Yes, it is, but unexpected problems can pop up. Title insurance is a cheap way to avoid the cost of major problems that could occur. Even if you're purchasing an REO property from a lender, get title insurance so you won't lose out if a lien was not properly recorded against a property or if you missed something when you researched the title.

Here is the bottom line: The more you know about a property's title and the more you watch out for potential red flags, the less likely you are to fail to get good title. And always get title insurance to protect yourself from loss.

 Although we recommend that you learn to inspect the title and chain of title yourself, for your first few properties and whenever you have doubts, we also recommend that you order a *title commitment* from the title company. A title commitment is not insurance. It is simply a preliminary report that lays out the title information in an easier-to-read format. Your title company may either charge for this service or offer it for free with the understanding that when you buy title insurance, you will buy it from them.

MYTH # **54**

I'll Have to Pay the Back Taxes and Insurance.

Fact: While You May Have to Pay Back Taxes, You Don't Have to Pay for Insurance—But You Should

We cover buying an insurance policy to cover the property in Myth #56. For now, just know that once you've purchased the property you should always get insurance, even if you aren't yet in physical possession. (But the fact remains: You are not *required* to purchase insurance.)

Whether you owe back taxes will depend on the stage of foreclosure at which you purchase the property. If you purchase in pre-foreclosure, back taxes are technically the responsibility of the homeowner. But if a tax lien has been applied to the property, you will want to pay the taxes to clear the title—otherwise the tax lien will stand in your way. If you buy at the foreclosure auction, you'll also want to take care of tax liens.

REO properties are a little different. By purchasing the property at the foreclosure auction, the lender has eliminated any liability of other liens that may be attached. You will not owe back taxes, and the title—except in very unusual circumstances—should be clear.

 Make sure no other investor has purchased a tax lien or deed against the property, which could supersede your interest in the property. You can check for this during your analysis stage by checking the county tax assessor or treasurer's office.

MYTH # **55**

I Can't Force the Previous Owners to Vacate the Property.

Fact: By Filing for an Eviction You Can Have the Sheriff Evict the Previous Owners, but You Are Often Better off Trying to Get Them to Move out Voluntarily

In states with no redemption period, once you have purchased the property, you are the owner, and the homeowners have no legal right to remain on the premises. If there is a redemption period, once the term has expired, the homeowners must leave. Some will already be gone by this time, while others will remain. As the new owner, it is now your responsibility to see that they leave.

Eviction is no fun—not for you and not for the people being evicted. When a sheriff or bailiff forcibly evicts a family, he and his crew show up and physically remove all of the family's belongings and set them out in the street. Neighbors usually come out to watch and may even pick through the belongings as if they were free for the taking. It is usually very humiliating for the family.

We recommend you do everything possible to work with the homeowners and encourage them to voluntarily vacate. We've offered incentives like the use of a dumpster, a moving van, or even some cash to help previous owners vacate as humanely as possible. Do we have to offer help? Legally, no; but put yourself in their shoes. How would you feel if the situation were reversed?

Some still will not leave, and that's when you need help. File the eviction papers at the local courthouse. Make sure you make copies of important documents, including your purchase agreement and any other documents pertaining to the sale. In some areas, the process starts with a trespassing notice; you'll be assigned a court date, and a judge will hear the case. Unless the homeowners successfully provide a legal reason why they need more time, the judge will typically set a date by which they must vacate.

If they do not comply, you'll have to call the sheriff and have the homeowners evicted. The sheriff goes to the property and removes the homeowners' belongings (typically placing them at the curb) or will keep the peace while *you* remove their belongings. (The process is different in different areas, so ask what you can expect when you file the eviction notice.)

While the sheriff will help you, our advice is to avoid formal eviction if you can. Some homeowners take their frustration out on the property. Your insurance policy may cover the damage, but it will still take time and effort to repair the property. If you can, help the homeowners move out peaceably by:

- **Providing extra time:** Some homeowners may have legitimate reasons why moving out on time will be difficult— illness, death in the family, or some other circumstance. If you wish, you can agree on a date they will move out, but make sure you create a formal document stating that commitment, and have them sign it. If they do not move out, you'll need that document when you file the trespassing notice.
- **Providing a moving van:** If the homeowners claim they don't have the means, hire a vehicle for them. Your goal is to remove as many objections or issues as you can.
- **Providing a dumpster:** You can help the homeowners clean up by providing a free dumpster (or roll-off container); doing so may keep you from having to throw their trash and unwanted items away yourself.

- **Providing free storage:** Some homeowners will claim they have nowhere to put their belongings. Arrange to prepay for storage space for a few months, but don't enter into an open-ended agreement; you don't want to be stuck paying the bill for years to come.
- **Providing cash:** Homeowners in foreclosure are by definition suffering financial hardship and may not have the funds to make a deposit on an apartment or afford the expenses of moving. But instead of providing the funds up front, make your agreement conditional upon them moving out on the specified date and leaving the premises clean and in good repair.

One last note: You can handle the eviction process yourself, but we recommend getting the help of your attorney. See it as insurance; you may spend a little more on attorney's fees, but you could save thousands on unexpected legal issues.

STOP Don't attempt to evict the previous owners yourself. Always call the sheriff, even if you're using the sheriff only as backup. You can never be sure what will happen. The homeowners could become angry or even violent, neighbors could try to walk off with some of the family's belongings, or the homeowners could try to accuse you of wrongdoing. With the sheriff on the scene, you have someone who can keep the peace and act as a witness that you did nothing wrong.

MYTH # **56**

I Don't Need Insurance Until the Previous Owners Move Out and I Take Possession of the Property.

Fact: You Need to Insure the Property Immediately After Purchasing It

Why? If the house burns to the ground during the redemption period, and you're not insured, you could lose your entire investment.

Once you have purchased the property, the previous homeowner's insurance is no longer in effect and does not cover the home for loss or damage. Even if it's still in the redemption period, the property is "yours" and you're responsible for damage, as well as taxes, as we noted earlier. While technically you don't have to pay insurance, you should. Otherwise, if a fire occurs, it's your loss. (Don't look for help from the homeowners; they're not going to redeem a property that no longer exists.)

Insurance will be relatively expensive during the redemption period. The agent usually won't be able to inspect the interior of the property, so she will have to estimate some key value factors and, to protect herself, will estimate high. But that's okay—better a higher insurance bill than a massive loss after a fire or storm.

In addition to threats from storms, floods, and other natural disasters, there is also a chance that the homeowners will trash the premises or gut the property. Angry homeowners have been known to move out and take everything that wasn't nailed down (and some stuff that was) with them. In some cases, they may take the furnace, kitchen cabinets and countertops, sinks, and even light fixtures. Just imagine what you could stand to lose by not having property insurance.

SECTION 7

Cashing In!

O kay, you own the property. Now what? You want to make a profit on your investment! Many investors get so caught up in the details and what they *think* should happen that they forget about the end goal—making a profit. In this section, we look at several myths that, if ignored, will end up costing you all that time and effort you've put in so far. Let's blow up some more myths and look at the bottom line: putting cash in your pocket!

MYTH # **57**

I Need to Finish Renovations Before I Sell.

Fact: Many Foreclosures Are Resold to Other Investors or Potential Homeowners with No Renovations at All

Most areas have no shortage of investors looking to buy investment properties, but many don't know how to find opportunities or aren't willing to do the work necessary to find them. Some are part-time investors who hold full-time jobs. They have cash to invest and resources to rehab a property, but they don't have time to find properties, evaluate opportunities, work with homeowners in the pre-foreclosure stage, and attend auctions.

If you enjoy the hunt for foreclosures and are good at it, you can cash in without taking on the hassle of rehabbing and selling the home. You simply track down opportunities, buy them, and then turn around and sell them to investors for a slight markup. Once you establish yourself as a *bird dog*, you'll have a ready source of investors interested in taking wholesale properties off your hands—and by spending very little of your own cash.

The process of finding properties and quickly reselling them to investors is frequently called *wholesaling*. The advantages of wholesaling are simple: You don't have to spend time and money performing repairs or renovations; you make money finding great opportunities for other investors. On the other hand, you won't make as much money on each deal, and you could find yourself owning a house that you can't find an investor to buy.

You can also decide to sell to another investor after you've made repairs but before you've renovated the property. Say you find a property in desperate need of cosmetic repairs: paint, carpet, and landscaping. It's also the smallest house in the neighborhood, and if you built an addition you could bring its value in line with the other houses and make a handsome profit on that investment. The problem is that you only have $15,000 to spend in total, and you need to sell the house relatively quickly before holding costs overwhelm you.

You could sell to another investor right away, but the property won't show well and as a result will not sell for as high an amount as possible. A better option might be to invest $10,000 in carpet, paint, and basic landscaping, saving $5,000 for holding costs or contingency. Then, when you show the house to an investor, he will be better able to see the potential in the property and pay a premium as a result. You may be able to double or even triple your $10,000 repairs investment.

Selling before all (or any) renovations are complete may reduce your profits, but it will also save you time and keep your investment costs low. In fact, if you have very little cash to invest, this might be your only option to profit on the deal. Later, when you've built up your investment funds, you will have more options to choose from.

 Doing a quick-cheap-and-easy rehab on a property is something we refer to as *whiteboxing*. Your goal is not to transform the property into a showcase home to sell to consumers. Instead, you transform the home into a clean, white box. This requires replacing any old or damaged carpet or flooring, painting the entire interior with neutral colors, thoroughly cleaning the entire home, and replacing all light fixtures and outlet covers.

MYTH # **58**

The More I Put into a Property, the More Return I'll Get.

Fact: Making the Right Renovations Will Generate the Most Return

You've heard that improvements to kitchens and bathrooms tend to pay off. (And you're right.) You've purchased a small but clean, well-maintained, three-bedroom ranch in a neighborhood with houses of similar size and condition. You want the property to make a splash when you list it, so you decide to spend $75,000 on marble countertops, granite floors, a custom shower, high-end faucets and fixtures, and, the *pièce-de-résistance*, a Sub-Zero built-in refrigerator-freezer.

The problem is that every other house in the neighborhood has Formica countertops, standard fixtures and bathroom components, and linoleum floors. Yours will certainly make a splash, but no one will pay a premium for the renovations you've made.

Items like wine cellars, dedicated gyms, tennis courts, and swimming pools seldom yield anything close to a good return on investment unless those things are the norm in the neighborhood and buyers expect them. Even so, the expense is seldom recoverable: You may spend $30,000 installing a swimming pool that adds only $10,000 to the sale price of the home.

Here's the key: Rehab a home to bring it up to or slightly above market standards, not to grossly exceed those standards. That's why you spent time checking out the neighborhood and being an expert in your area. If you're not sure what the other homes in the neighborhood are like and what improvements will make a real difference, ask your real estate agent for advice. Avoid any temptation to overimprove.

Your goal is to make the property more attractive to buyers. A clean, attractive property in good repair sells more easily, because buyers can easily picture themselves living or working there. In addition, they can move in immediately without sinking a lot of time and effort into costly repairs and renovations. An attractive property is clean, well-maintained, and has an appeal buyers can't miss.

Perform only fix-ups or improvements that are visible. Painting, installing new carpet, refinishing wood floors, and installing new bathroom fixtures adds real, visible value to the property. Adding extra insulation to an attic will not. Buyers may appreciate your energy-saving gesture if they somehow manage to notice it, but they'll never pay a higher price for your efforts.

Also stay away from structural work if you can. Costs can easily get out of hand as soon as you start to modify the structure or systems of the house. The easiest and most profitable fix-ups are ones that don't require major structural changes. If you can, avoid moving kitchen and bathroom plumbing, opening up load-bearing walls, or adding rooms outside the original footprint of the home—unless, of course, the renovation will more than pay for itself.

You want the property to be in good repair, but buyers don't expect perfection. Say you bought a foreclosure property at auction, and the shingle roof is about 10 years old. The shingles are slightly faded, but no torn or cracked shingles are evident. Still, you're convinced you can increase the curb appeal by replacing the roof.

That's a bad idea. The average roof lasts for at least 15 years, and since in this case there are no signs of damage, the roof should easily pass a home inspection. Depending on the size of the house, you could spend anywhere from $5,000 to $10,000 or more replacing the roof. A buyer will never pay a premium for a brand-new roof. It might look more attractive, but the house won't sell for a higher price. Giving the buyers a new roof in this case would be like reaching into your pocket, pulling out $5,000 to $10,000, and handing it to the buyers.

Improvements to kitchens and bathrooms usually cost quite a bit but will also pay back the most. They're the two types of rooms that buyers look at the most critically. Even buyers on tight budgets want the best possible kitchen and bathrooms they can afford. Real estate investors rarely buy houses they don't spend time and money on improving the kitchens and bathrooms.

The upgrades in a kitchen can range from basic cosmetics like paint, flooring, and appliances to expanding the kitchen into an adjoining room and replacing everything from the ceiling to the floor and all the cabinets and appliances.

Even buyers of a two-bedroom home expect at least a full bath and a half bath to solve the crunch when everyone is getting ready for work and school in the morning. If you can turn a one-bathroom house into a two-bathroom house by using existing space, you'll likely recover your investment.

In bathrooms, the upgrades can be as basic as scrubbing and wallpapering or as extensive as demolishing and rebuilding with a new bathtub and shower, vanity and countertop, tile, and lighting.

If you plan to live in the house, and the neighborhood supports a luxury bathroom or a gourmet kitchen, you may be able to rationalize the expense; after all, you'll get to enjoy those renovations as well as hope they pay off down the road. Still, do some research and find out if comparable properties featuring high-end upgrades will sell for prices that cover the cost of significant renovations.

Here are some ways you can give any property an inexpensive and quick makeover:

Freshen the Exterior

- Mow and edge the lawn.
- Trim trees and shrubs.
- Replace dead or dying shrubs and plant flowers, especially near the front of the house (to improve curb appeal).
- Apply a fresh layer of mulch.
- Remove any clutter or eyesores.
- Fill driveway or sidewalk cracks.
- Power wash siding or paint wood siding.
- Remove window air conditioning units (they may cool the house but they're unattractive).
- Repair or replace windows and screens.
- Add, replace, or paint shutters.

- Paint the front door and trim (the front door makes a huge impression).
- Replace gutters (preferably with seamless gutters).
- Replace exterior light fixtures, and make sure all bulbs are in working order.

Gussy up the Interior

- Clean every surface.
- Wash windows.
- Install new window blinds or shades.
- Clean or replace drapes and curtains.
- Remove hooks and nails from the walls and patch the holes.
- Paint all rooms using flat, neutral colors (if in doubt, paint it white).
- Repair all doors and doorknobs and make sure each door opens and closes smoothly.
- Install new light-switch and outlet cover plates.
- Install new smoke detectors.
- Replace carpeting and refinish or replace damaged or worn flooring.

Tidy up the Kitchen

- Install a new stainless-steel sink.
- Install a new faucet.
- Replace old or worn countertops.
- Refinish or repaint cabinets and replace the knobs and handles.
- Put new contact paper on all cabinet shelves and drawers.

Scour the Bathrooms

- Install a new vanity.
- Install all new fixtures.
- Replace the toilet seat.
- Replace towel hangers.
- Replace shower curtains, or better yet, install shower doors.
- Apply fresh caulk around the edges and base of the tub, shower, sink, and toilet.
- Scrub the grout between any tile work.

Spiff up the Bedrooms

- Paint.
- Recarpet.
- Replace light fixtures.
- Install closet organizers to make a small space more roomy.

Make Unfinished Basements Livable

- Sweep out cobwebs and dust ductwork, pipes, or wiring.
- Seal any wall cracks.
- Paint concrete or block walls with a white sealing paint.
- Paint or tile concrete floors.

Take Care of Mechanicals

- Change furnace filters.
- Clean or replace hot-water tanks.
- Repair any leaky faucets.
- Unclog any slow drains.
- Consider having heating or air conditioning systems checked by a professional.

Your goal is to eliminate anything that is undesirable or unsightly. Some prospective buyers will merely take a cursory glance at the property, while others will check *everything*. Ensuring the little things are in great shape inspires confidence in a homebuyer. The house doesn't need to be the *best* home in the neighborhood; to sell it quickly and for a reasonable profit your goal is to make it the *cleanest*.

Whatever repairs, renovations, or improvements you plan to make, be sure they meet local building-code requirements. Violations can easily give potential buyers second thoughts about the property, not to mention a legal reason to back out of a contract if you've reached one.

MYTH # **59**

I'll Save Money and Make More Profit If I Make All Repairs and Upgrades Myself.

Fact: Profit Is the Result of a Number of Factors, Including Time

We all like to save money, but it's easy to be pennywise and dollar foolish.

Let's use a very simple example. Say you've purchased a foreclosure property and you want to paint the bedroom before you sell it because you can save $300 by not hiring a painter. (We told you it would be simple.) You arranged a hard-money loan with a lender, and your monthly payment is $1,000. (You have other holding costs, such as insurance, taxes, utilities, and so on, but we'll limit our consideration to the cost of the hard-money loan for the purposes of this exercise.)

You have the best intentions, but you're incredibly busy and it takes you a couple months to free up the time to paint the bedroom. You did manage to save $300, but now you're two months farther down the road and you've spent $2,000 in loan payments. If by having the room painted by a professional you could have sold the house two months sooner, you would have enjoyed a $1,700 return on your $300 investment.

If you're already extremely busy, handling repairs and renovations on your own probably doesn't make good financial sense. The more work you do yourself, the more money you can make—but not if you don't have time to actually *do* the work and the skills to do it well.

In addition, repairs and renovations that are not up to the neighborhood's standards will not only yield a lower return, they may also make potential buyers wonder what *else* might be wrong with the house. When you're selling, your goal is to attract as many potential buyers as possible, not scare them away with shoddy craftsmanship. If you don't have the skills to do the work right, either invest time and money in gaining those skills or hire someone else.

Here are some rules of thumb:

- **If you don't have the time, hire someone else.** If you're evaluating a foreclosure property for purchase, estimate the repairs and renovations you'll need to do and match that with the time you have available. If you need to hire contractors or other skilled labor, simply factor those costs into your evaluation.

- **If you don't have the skills, hire someone else.** Or consider taking on small jobs to build your skills. Don't try to build a perimeter stone wall if you're not a mason; start with a small patio project. You may learn a lot by taking on a big job, but the meter will be running while you do—and it's *your* meter that's running.
- **Evaluate the per-hour cost.** Say you're a lawyer with an hourly rate of $150. You have all the clients you can handle. Would you spend eight hours cutting the grass and trimming trees and bushes if you could pay a landscaper $20 an hour while you attend to your clients and bill at $150 per hour? Hire out jobs that make sense; if you have good electrical skills, replace wiring or fixtures to avoid $30-an-hour electrician rates while you pay a local teenager $8 an hour to cut grass and clean up the yard. (This sounds obvious, but you would be surprised to know how many people make this simple mistake.)
- **Factor in holding costs.** You can save money doing the work yourself, but the longer it takes you to get the house ready for sale, the higher your holding costs will be. Compare the cost of hiring an expert with the holding costs you stand to save. If you can save money by bringing in the pros, do it!

Don't forget to factor in the value of time spent with your family and friends. Real estate investing can be a lifelong pursuit. Don't commit yourself to working 20-hour days at your full-time job and your foreclosure projects. Spending time with your family is just as important as any investment opportunity. Balance your work and your home life, and over the long term you and your family will be much happier.

If you enjoy and are skilled at finding and buying investment properties that are packed with potential, but you're not so good at fixing up the properties or contracting, then consider partnering with someone who has the skills you are missing. Just be sure that you have a detailed, written agreement that stipulates all the conditions of your partnership. Hire an attorney to help you craft your partnership agreement.

MYTH # **60**

I Can't Make a Profit.

Fact: Maybe You Can if You Look Closely Enough

Every deal doesn't offer an obvious opportunity.

A few years ago, a friend of ours was evaluating a possible foreclosure purchase. The property in question was a small house just a couple of streets over from a university. The owners rented the house to students. The house was in decent shape, but since it was used for student housing, it was by no means in pristine condition. The owners owed only $70,000, and our friend felt he could probably purchase the property for $110,000.

Due to its location, comparable nearby properties were selling for approximately $115,000 to $120,000. The chances to profit were small, because holding and closing costs—and the real estate commission—would easily eat up any potential profit. He started to walk away from the deal but decided to give it a closer look when the owners said they would be interested in selling during the foreclosure stage. (Many owners will sell investment or rental properties more readily during foreclosure, since that sale does not affect their own personal housing situation.)

First he checked out the existing tenant leases. The property contained two apartments, and the current rent payments would barely cover his loan payments, making the property cash-flow negative (meaning more money would be spent on loan payments and expenses than would be received in the form of rent payments from tenants.) On closer inspection, though, he realized that the owners had not raised the rent in 10 years, and the apartments were renting for almost 40% less than comparable local units. In addition, both leases were due to expire in two months, meaning he could start charging market rates at that time. (When a property changes hands, the existing leases remain in force even if the new owner was not a signatory to the lease. When existing leases expire, the new owner can charge whatever the market will bear.)

He then checked out a detached garage on the property filled with junk. The tenants would not be willing to pay a premium to garage their cars, but they may be willing to pay extra for the convenience of additional storage space.

Then he looked at the lot itself. The property line extended all the way to a street at the back edge of the property. Parking at the nearby university was at a premium, and many students had to park almost a mile away from the campus. He felt he could add six to eight parking spots at the back of the property and charge for their use on a monthly basis. (Other neighbors were already providing students with a similar service.)

After he factored in the increase in revenue due to market-level rent amounts, charging a premium for onsite storage space, and charging commuters for parking, he realized that he could pay $110,000 for the property and still generate positive cash flow of $500 per month.

Each opportunity is different. In some cases, no matter how hard you look, you won't see opportunities for profit. If that's the case, walk away and find a better opportunity. Evaluate, estimate, and ask for advice. In the end, don't enter any deal when you're not confident you can make a profit. But at the same time, don't walk away too quickly. Take the time to look for what others may have missed.

 Many real estate investors consider a buy-and-hold strategy to be much more profitable over the long-term than a buy-fix-sell (flipping) strategy, because it offers more ways to earn money. In addition to earning money when you sell the property, you earn additional profits, because while the property's value is appreciating, your renters are paying down the principal on your mortgage loan. In addition, you get a tax deduction for property depreciation.

MYTH # **61**

I Won't Be Able to Sell It—They Couldn't!

Fact: Find the Right Agent, Make Repairs and Renovations that Make Sense, and Price the Property Realistically for a Reasonably Rapid Sale

Some homeowners realize, even before the foreclosure process begins, that they're over their heads financially. Instead of waiting for a bad situation to get worse, they may try to sell the house. If you're paying attention to your local real estate market—and you should be—you may notice the house is on the market even though at the time you're not interested.

Say that happens, and then six months or even a year later you see a foreclosure notice for the same property. Many investors feel they should steer clear of the property; if it sat on the market that long, *something* must be wrong, right?

Right, but the "something" may be a factor you can easily control and overcome:

- Some real estate agents do a better job marketing their clients' homes. (We discussed finding a good real estate agent in Myth #9.) Some agents know how to market to potential buyers of different types of properties. Some have contacts and have built a local network of real estate investors who may be interested in the property. Some, quite simply, will work harder on the seller's behalf. It's very possible the homeowner's listing agent simply put the home on the Multiple Listing Service and hoped for the best.
- The listing price could have been too high. In a flat or a down market, pricing a home at or above full market value usually (but not always) means the house will take a relatively long time to sell. Houses priced slightly below market value have a much greater chance of selling more quickly. A listing price is simply a reflection of what a homeowner hopes the house will sell for; its value isn't determined until the house actually sells. (Remember the concept of ready, willing, and able buyers.) And it may seem a strange phenomenon, but houses that have been on the market for a long time due to a too-high listing price will still sit even if the homeowners drop the price significantly—even to below-market-value levels. Many homeowners assume they can start high and then drop the price if no one is interested, but that strategy can often backfire.
- Simple repairs have been neglected. Believe it or not, Ralph has taken potential buyers to see homes with torn window screens, front doors that won't quite close, and huge stains smack in the middle

of the living room floor. Those houses make a first impression—a *terrible* first impression. Curb appeal, the first impression the home makes when potential buyers drive up, is absolutely critical. Houses with obvious defects are very difficult to sell.

- ◆ Obvious renovations have not been made. Orange shag carpet may have been quite the rage in the 1970s, but today it will cause buyers to turn tail and run. Outdated appliances, seventies-style linoleum, and shrubs that threaten to swallow up the front of the house turn potential buyers away. A few thousand dollars spent on obvious upgrades can make the difference between a quick sale and a long spell on the market. Homeowners who are struggling financially may not be able to afford repairs and renovations.

In all likelihood, the owners tried to sell the property at a premium to help them escape their financial difficulties. The key to successful real estate investing is to aim for a reasonable profit so you can sell each property relatively quickly and with less risk.

Don't try to make a killing on every deal, and remember, your profits are determined by the price you paid, not by what you sold the property for. Pay the right price and your profits are basically assured; pay too much, and no effort or further investment will help you make a profit.

Evaluate each possibility and focus on setting a realistic walk-away price, make sensible repairs and renovations, list the property with a good real estate agent, and aim for a reasonable profit.

Investors often try to trim costs by selling the property themselves. Their reasoning is, Why pay a 6 to 7% commission to an agent when you can sell it yourself and keep the entire profit? Keep in mind that a top-producing real estate agent can usually sell a home in half the time and for more money than you can sell it yourself. The agent may save you more on holding costs and get you a higher price—more than paying for her 6 to 7% commission. In addition, by delegating the task of selling the property to someone else, you have more time to pursue other investment opportunities.

MYTH # **62**

I Already Have a Home; My Best Bet Is to Flip the Foreclosures I Purchase.

Fact: What You Do with Each Property Depends on Your Situation and Your Goals

First, let's get something out of the way. Except under very special circumstances, you should always invest in a personal residence before you invest in other opportunities. Homeownership provides a number of tax advantages, lets you benefit from appreciation, and provides you with a place you can call your own. (Besides, why pay someone else's mortgage?) So, unless you plan to move out of the area in the next year, or a foreclosure opportunity pops up that makes a great investment but you don't want to live in that area, first buy a house you will live in.

Now that we've gotten that out of the way, flipping foreclosures is not the only way to make money. Many investors buy and hold properties to rent to others.

You can also buy a house that someone else will pay for. While that sounds impossible, it happens every day. If you own rental property, someone else makes your mortgage payments for you, and you enjoy the benefits. If you buy a foreclosure and rent it to others, their rent payments should cover your loan expenses, taxes, insurance, and other costs. (If your rental income does not bring in more than your expenses, then your cash flow is negative, and you should probably not purchase the property unless you have ideas for how to generate additional rental income or lower your costs. See Myth #60 for a few ideas.)

There are four major advantages to owning rental property:

1. Your tenants pay your loans.
2. You deduct your loan interest from your taxable income.
3. You enjoy positive cash flow from your rental properties by collecting more in rent than you pay for the loan, taxes, insurance, and other expenses.
4. You increase your net worth as your loan balance decreases and the property's value increases.

You can also purchase a property to live in even if you already own a home. Let's say you buy a foreclosure property in need of repairs and renovations. You have the skills to perform the work, but you don't have tons of free time. You could purchase the property, move in, and do the renovations at your own pace. Holding costs are no longer an issue, because you have to live somewhere—why not there? You can take your time, do the work right, save money on the renovations, and increase your profits when you eventually sell. Plus you'll enjoy tax advantages.

Here's why. If you live in the home, you may be exempt from capital gains taxes when you sell, even if you own more than one home.

Roughly speaking, if you live in your home for two out of five years, you're exempt from paying capital gains tax. (If you live in the home for two consecutive years, you qualify; "two out of five" is used to qualify people who own multiple residences.) If you buy a foreclosure property for $150,000, live in it while you spend $40,000 renovating it, and sell it four years later for $400,000, the $210,000 profit you make is exempt from taxes. (See Figure 7.1.) You pay no taxes on that gain as long as you purchase another house within six months from the date of sale. You can make up to $250,000 on the transaction or $500,000 if you're married; anything over those amounts is taxable. Then again, if you can make over $300,000 on a deal in just a few years, possibly you shouldn't complain about paying taxes on the $50,000 you made over the exemption amount!

You can use the personal residence exemption over and over again. The tax savings can help you buy more expensive properties and move you up the homeownership ladder. Some real estate investors who own multiple

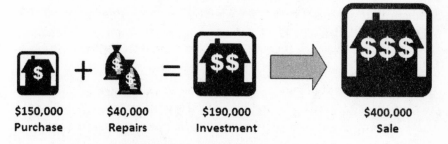

| $150,000 Purchase | $40,000 Repairs | $190,000 Investment | $400,000 Sale |

$210,000 Tax-Free Profits!

Figure 7.1 Buying a Foreclosure as a Personal Residence

properties continue to move into a new personal residence every two or three years just so they can take advantage of the tax exemption.

 In a slow market, it is sometimes wise to list both your investment property and your personal residence for sale. If your residence sells first, you can then move into the investment property. Admittedly, this isn't an option in all situations, but it is certainly something to think about when you're facing the painful reality of trying to maintain two properties.

MYTH # **63**

The Property Will Be Easiest to Flip When It's Market Ready.

Fact: You May Have a Better Chance of Selling the Property During the Renovation Stage

Everyone likes a good deal. And people love to get in early, hence the popularity of after-Thanksgiving sales when stores open at 6 A.M. or even earlier. When you buy a foreclosure property and start to make repairs or renovations, you'll find that the neighbors are fascinated—not only by the changes you're making to the house and how that affects the neighborhood, but also by the fact that you're obviously treating the purchase as an investment. You'll find that some neighbors will "accidentally" wander by to introduce themselves and see what you're doing. Others will want to check out the work taking place, because they would like to make changes to their own homes, and if nothing else, would like to live vicariously through your efforts.

Don't ignore the neighbors or other visitors. Every person you meet could potentially buy the property, or refer a buyer to you. Don't talk about what you paid for the house or how much you're spending; simply say you're working hard to make sure the property is safe, clean, well-maintained, and in move-in condition for the next owner. If a visitor asks what you'll list the property for, at this point say you're not sure. An honest and candid answer could be, "You know, I'm not sure. We've finalized about 90% of our renovation plans, but we are still considering a few options, so I'm not sure yet what a fair price will be. All I'm sure of right now is that we're putting a lot of money and effort into the property."

Conversations like these can often create some premarket buzz that generates interest even before renovations are complete. Some buyers may want to get in early and purchase the property before you've invested a lot in renovations, so they can pay less for the property; save money by performing renovations themselves; and pick out the carpet, paint, and other materials themselves.

Don't overlook the neighbors. A friend of ours has sold several properties to neighbors; each was an older couple who wanted to buy a house for their grown children to live in (conveniently located right down the street from their parents). Just like during the foreclosure purchase stage, don't worry about where you stand in the repair and renovation process when you sell: If you can make a reasonable profit and you're happy with the deal, then sell. A buyer in the hand is always worth two buyers in the bush.

Work on the exterior first, or start the exterior renovations at the same time you begin renovating the interior. This can generate a great deal of word-of-mouth advertising. Remember that neighbors would really like to have a say in who lives in the neighborhood. If someone they know and like is looking for a home, the neighbors will tell them about the home that's currently being fixed up in the neighborhood. If you still haven't sold the home by the time renovations are complete, hold an open house, and be sure to invite all the neighbors.

MYTH # **64**

It's a Foreclosure; I'll Still Make a $10,000 Profit!

Fact: The Profit You Make Is the Difference Between All Your Costs and Your Eventual Selling Price—That's the Only Calculation You Can Count On

You can get great deals and make fabulous profits from foreclosures. (You certainly won't on every deal, though, despite the claims of get-rich-quick real estate investment "gurus.") But there is never a guarantee of profit, much less a minimum guaranteed profit amount. A foreclosure investment is like any other investment:

Selling Price − All Costs = Profit

We've covered the profit analysis equation before, but the point bears repeating. You make a profit only if you sell the property for more than all your costs: the purchase price, loan payments, fees, taxes, insurance, repairs, renovations, real estate commissions, even the value of your time. If you spend more than you sell for, you lose money. It's that simple.

It's true that foreclosure properties are often great deals; you can frequently buy a property for significantly less than its market value. Yet your profits are in no way assured just because you purchased the property at a low price at auction. The fact that you couldn't inspect the house beforehand is a risk: The homeowners could have failed to maintain the property or purposely damaged it out of anger, frustration, or spite. Major environmental problems could exist; a buried, leaking oil tank in the backyard, for example, could cost thousands of dollars to remove and environmentally remediate. Foreclosure properties bought at auction are purchased as is, and if major problems exist, those problems are yours.

Even if you can inspect the property and have a well-reasoned estimate of the repair and renovation costs needed, changes in the real estate market could torpedo home prices. In a matter of months, the home you felt sure you could sell for $200,000 may have a market value of $190,000 or less; if you estimated you would make $10,000 in profit, that profit has disappeared. To protect yourself and ensure you've created a buffer against unforeseen expenses, always factor in these costs:

- ◆ Repair and renovation expenses.
- ◆ Holding costs: property taxes, loan interest, insurance, utilities, and so on. Calculate the holding costs for the entire time it will take to make repairs and renovations, to wait out the redemption period, and the time you and your agent estimate it will take to sell the property.

- Real estate commissions (when you sell).
- Transfer taxes.
- Fees for title research and any other documents.
- Recording fees.
- Miscellaneous expenses.
- Profit. While profit isn't an expense, you should factor in an amount for what you hope to make. Plan to make at least 20% on every deal—more if possible.

Have you ever heard the expression, "The car is not sold until the cash is in my hand"? Well, a profit is not assured until the purchase price is in your hand—and the purchase price is greater than all your costs.

Don't let your expectations get out of hand. Overestimate expenses and underestimate profits so you are not disappointed by the outcome. Being pleasantly surprised beats being disappointed.

MYTH # **65**

I Should Feel Guilty.

Fact: By Treating the Homeowners with Compassion and a Sense of Fairness, You Offer Them a Valuable Service

Many people avoid investing in foreclosures because they feel they are taking advantage of someone else's misfortune. It's an understandable emotion; none of us wants to profit from the hardship of others.

But as we stated way back in Myth #1, there is no logical reason you should feel guilty. Foreclosure laws and processes exist to protect homeowners. Laws give homeowners the opportunity to find ways to overcome their financial difficulties and keep their homes. If you try to buy a property in pre-foreclosure, the homeowner will agree only if the deal makes sense to her. (In fact, the homeowner may see you as a financial savior if you buy her home during pre-foreclosure.) In states with legally mandated redemption periods, homeowners get additional time to reverse their fortunes even after the property has been auctioned. Homeowners who cannot make their payments or redeem their property will lose their home no matter what you do.

Here's the bottom line: If you don't buy the property at auction or as an REO property, someone else will. It no longer belongs to the homeowner. No matter what you do, the homeowners won't get their property back; it's too late for that to occur.

As long as you're not defrauding homeowners, you are simply playing the role of investor purchasing a property that the homeowners can no longer afford.

In fact, buyers of foreclosure properties are an important part of the real estate financing process. Lenders need to sell foreclosure properties; without buyers their losses mount. Creditors are often repaid by foreclosure sale proceeds. While foreclosure is certainly an unfortunate outcome for a homeowner in financial distress, it is a necessary outcome to ensure the health of the financial institutions that make loans to homeowners, and the health of other creditors, contractors, and real estate professionals.

You can also help the homeowners in other ways:

- ◆ Provide financial advice. If you're not a financial professional, don't represent yourself as one. But you can help homeowners in distress by suggesting they consider:
  - ○ Consolidating debts to reduce monthly payments
  - ○ Creating a realistic budget to help them get their spending under control
  - ○ Negotiating with lenders to restructure payments or explore other options
  - ○ Refinancing or selling the property
- ◆ Assist homeowners in a job search. Some homeowners are in distress due to a job loss. If they need a job and you know of openings, give them a hand.
- ◆ Suggest they seek help from family and friends. Even though they may be able to save the property with help from their family, causing you to miss out on a potential deal, you'll have the satisfaction of knowing you made a real difference in someone's life.

- Suggest selling the house before foreclosure. You may lose the chance to buy the property, but you'll have gained a friend (and a possible source of referrals) for life.

While we're at it, here are some things you should *never* do:

- Withhold information from the homeowners that could help them sell the house themselves and save some of their equity in the property.
- Mislead homeowners into thinking their only option is to sell to you.
- Befriend the homeowners so they'll sell the property to you, even though doing so is not in their best interest.
- Buy the tax lien and then convince the homeowners to move out because you "own the property," even though they could simply pay the back taxes and retain possession.
- Buy a property at auction and then tell the homeowners they have to move out immediately, even though their state grants them the opportunity to redeem the property during the redemption period.

If you suspect that what you're saying to homeowners is not in their best interest, in all likelihood you're doing something wrong. While you want to make a profit, you don't want to do so by misrepresenting facts.

Present yourself professionally, act in good faith, uphold the highest ethical standards, and follow the rules and guidelines of the foreclosure process. If you do, you will not take advantage of anyone; instead you may be helping someone recover from a terrible situation.

 As you gain experience in the foreclosure market in your area, you will no doubt encounter "investors" who are committed to taking advantage of homeowners. Another valuable service you may provide to homeowners is warning them about these con artists. Eventually, with your assistance, word will spread and hopefully put these con artists out of business or at least force them to change their tactics.

SECTION 8

Avoiding Disaster

How do you protect yourself from *yourself?* Once you've gotten into the foreclosure market, it's easy to take things for granted and let some things slip. Don't! Concentrating on these last few myths will save you a *lot* of heartache, not to mention an enormous amount of time, energy, and dollars.

MYTH # **66**

I'm an Experienced Real Estate Investor, So I Don't Need to Do My Homework.

Fact: Experienced and *Successful* Real Estate Investors Do the Most Homework

Every transaction is different. Every deal is different. No matter how long you've been investing, you'll run across something new. Ask an experienced real estate investor whether he is ever surprised anymore, and the answer will likely be some form of, "Every day."

Knowledge is the experienced investor's best insurance. Experienced investors double-check value estimates with members of their team. Experienced investors take a close look at the property. Experienced investors thoroughly inspect the title for mechanics liens, tax liens, second mortgages, and title chain pitfalls.

There are no shortcuts to success, especially in foreclosure investing. Work hard and do your homework and results will follow. Never rest on your laurels and assume you know everything you need to know about a property.

 Complacency in real estate investing is dangerous. The one time you fail to perform your due diligence and check the chain of title or purchase an insurance policy will be the one time that something goes wrong. Create a fail-safe system complete with checklists to make sure you have taken all the necessary steps before purchasing and taking possession of an investment property. Don't trust someone else to save you; this is *your* money you are investing.

MYTH # **67**

I Am Familiar with the House, So I Don't Need to Inspect It.

Fact: You *Always* Need to Know as Much as You Can about Every Property's Condition

Every property you consider should be inspected as thoroughly as you possibly can under the circumstances. Even if you can't get inside, you can assess the exterior, get a sense of the neighborhood, assess the quality of schools, and check out local crime rates.

Say a property is under foreclosure, but the homeowners are still in residence and don't want you to set foot on the property, much less inside the house for a look around. With camera and notebook in hand, from the street you can still evaluate:

+ The overall impression the property makes (curb appeal)
+ The condition of the paint or siding
+ The roof, gutters, and downspouts
+ The windows and doors
+ The driveway, landscaping, and any exterior structures

Check all four sides; unless the yard is very large or the house is surrounded by a tall fence, you can almost always walk around and see the majority of the house and the lot.

Immediate red flags include:

- **Standing water:** Standing water on the lot can be a sign of poor drainage and can also cause a wet basement or a settling or cracked foundation. Look for damp, mossy areas and areas where grass doesn't grow. Some drainage problems are easy to fix, but if you see standing water, make sure you investigate further.

- **Water and moisture damage:** Rain, snow, and moisture damage can be seen by wood rotting in the soffits, where there's no ventilation, or moss growing on roof shingles or siding. Signs of exterior moisture damage usually indicate damage inside the house as well, especially in attics. Dampness can also promote the growth of mold and mildew; mold creates health risks and is expensive to repair.

- **Structural problems:** Major structural problems, like a cracked or settling foundation, can be very expensive and time-consuming to repair. Unless you can get a firm estimate on repair costs and pay an appropriately low price for the property, don't consider it. Large cracks in walls, especially in corners, and long horizontal cracks can be a tip-off to foundation movement.

While you assess the house itself, also develop an overall impression of the property and its location. Try to determine whether the house has potential. If you make cosmetic improvements, will it appeal to a broad range of buyers? Will prospective buyers feel the neighborhood is attractive and a place they want to raise their families?

One of Ralph's rules of thumb is, "My eyes or no buys." In other words, he won't buy a property unless he sees it with his own eyes. You should follow the same approach.

 One of the benefits of meeting with the homeowners in preforeclosure is that it gives you the opportunity to see inside the home. Even if you ultimately purchase the property at auction, seeing inside can give you an edge over other investors who may be bidding on the property.

MYTH # **68**

The House Looks Great—It Won't Need Many Repairs!

Fact: No Matter How Much You Know, Always Leave Room for Contingencies

Every experienced foreclosure investor has a horror story or two to tell: the house that was trashed by previous owners, termite damage to the floor joists that cost thousands to fix, a heating system that died the day after the property was purchased. Any experienced foreclosure investor who hasn't been unpleasantly surprised is not, in fact, experienced.

To cover themselves from unexpected expenses, smart investors evaluate each deal using one or two worst-case scenarios. A *worst-case scenario* is exactly what it sounds like: Simply say, "What's the worst thing I can reasonably expect to happen?" Then estimate the cost associated with it.

For example, say you have not been able to inspect the interior of a foreclosure property. You can tell from looking at the house that it is approximately 1,500 square feet. You and your real estate agent determine, based on checking out comparables, that the house will be worth $155,000 if it's in good repair and condition, so you will price it at $150,000 to help it sell quickly. You have already determined that your acquisition costs, holding costs, basic repair costs, and closing costs when you sell (including real estate commission) add up to $25,000.

One worst-case scenario you could evaluate is if the homeowners smash holes in all the walls, tear out the toilets and sinks, and trash the carpets before they leave. Ask for cost estimates from a drywall contractor, a plumber, and your local carpet outlet. Homeowner's insurance won't cover this type of damage since it's intentional. So, say those costs add up to $20,000. If you can purchase the house for $105,000 and the worst-case scenario occurs, you will break even on the deal. (If the worst-case scenario doesn't occur, you earn a $20,000 bonus.)

Another worst-case scenario could involve holding costs. We'll use the same example as above. Say you determine your holding costs (loan payments, utilities, taxes, insurance, etc.) will be $2,000 per month. You plan to complete all repairs and renovations within a month and price the property slightly below market value; you hope it can sell within two months. So, you estimate you'll hold the property for three months, for total holding costs of $6,000.

What happens if the house doesn't sell, and you hold it for six additional months? Simple: Holding costs increase by $12,000 to a total of $18,000. Now, when you sell, you will make a profit of $8,000 rather than the $20,000 you hoped for.

Other common contingencies to plan for include other unexpected repair costs like replacing furnaces, appliances, or roofs, delays in evicting homeowners, or the effect of rising interest rates.

No matter how great the house looks, evaluate the deal by accounting for several worst-case scenarios. If you don't have cash reserves to draw on in case of emergencies, make sure that if the *worst* turns out to be true, you'll still earn a profit.

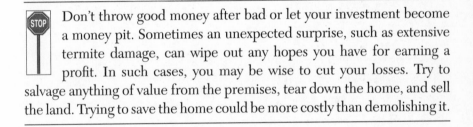 Don't throw good money after bad or let your investment become a money pit. Sometimes an unexpected surprise, such as extensive termite damage, can wipe out any hopes you have for earning a profit. In such cases, you may be wise to cut your losses. Try to salvage anything of value from the premises, tear down the home, and sell the land. Trying to save the home could be more costly than demolishing it.

MYTH # **69**

This House Is Amazing—It's Worth a Fortune!

Fact: Wishful Thinking Can Blind You and Cost You a Fortune

Getting input from experts is always important, but it's especially important if you think your emotions are running away with you. If your first look at a house causes your pulse rate to soar as you consider the possibilities, that's a sure sign you *need* a second opinion. Have your agent give you an objective estimate of the property's current value and, if it needs any work, its potential value once repairs and renovations are complete. Then, to be safe, take 5 to 10% off that estimate.

As we've mentioned before, the true value of a property is what a buyer is ready, willing, and able to pay. When you're considering properties to buy, you don't have that luxury, so you and the experts you rely on will estimate the value. Or you can have a formal appraisal performed; in most cases you won't, but having a good sense of how appraisals are performed can be helpful to investors and homeowners alike.

Property values are estimated using three basic types of appraisals: sales comparison, cost, and income capitalization. Let's look at each.

Sales Comparison. This method estimates the value of a property by comparing it to similar properties that recently sold in the area, called *comparables* or *comps*. An appraiser will compare comps to the subject property in order to determine its value. Sales comparison appraisals are typically used to evaluate single-family homes, townhouses, and duplexes.

Appraisers are generally required to compare the subject property to at least three comps. Since very few houses are identical, the appraiser will adjust the relative values according to standard formulas. For example, if the subject property has a swimming pool and a comp does not, the appraiser will adjust the value of the property being appraised higher to compensate for the additional feature.

Here's a simple example. Say you're interested in a four-bedroom, two-bath, 1,900-square-foot home built in 1975. A similar 1,900-square-foot, four-bedroom, two-bath home built in 1973, located two streets over in the same neighborhood, sold last week for $220,000. Roughly speaking, the house you're considering should sell for approximately the same price as the similar house a couple of streets away. The houses are the same size, have the same number of bedrooms and bathrooms, and are nearly the same age. As long as the two houses are in similar condition they should be comparable, and their values should be similar.

Keep in mind the appraiser has a reasonable amount of latitude within which to determine the value of the property. Two different appraisers evaluating the same property will rarely arrive at the same exact value.

Cost. The cost method determines the value of a property by determining how much it would cost to replace. The appraiser estimates the value of the property if it were new and then deducts an amount for depreciation, or wear and tear, based on the current condition of the property. The value of the land is determined by using recent sales of comps. Land value cannot be determined by the cost method since the land cannot be replaced.

Cost appraisals are more accurate when a property is fairly new, since less wear and tear has occurred, and it is easier to estimate the replacement cost. Cost appraisals are also useful when a property is fairly unique, and suitable comparables in the area can't be found.

Income Capitalization. Income capitalization appraisals place a value on a property based on its ability to produce income. Income capitalization appraisals are commonly used to estimate the value of office buildings, commercial real estate, and even residential rental properties. Very seldom is an income capitalization appraisal done by an appraiser; this type of estimate is usually done by an investor like you. In effect, your goal is to determine how much you're willing to pay based on how much the property will return in income.

The process is straightforward. Calculate the gross income or rent for the property, then subtract an amount for typical operating expenses like loan payments, taxes, maintenance, insurance, and other costs. The result is the net income you expect the property to generate per month or per year.

Here's a very simple example:

Gross income	$30,000
Expenses	$27,000
Net income	$3,000

Under this scenario, the property will produce $3,000 per year in net income. Now you can decide how much you're willing to pay for the property.

You can calculate the value by using the formula:

$$\text{Value} = \frac{\textbf{Net Income}}{\textbf{Capitalization Rate}}$$

The capitalization rate is the expected rate of return. Let's say in this case you want to get at least a 10% rate of return; if you can't, you'd rather invest your money elsewhere:

$$\text{Value} = \frac{\$3,000}{10\%}$$

So, the value of the property to you is $30,000. That's the most you can pay in order to get a 10% rate of return. In effect, that becomes the value of the property, at least as you wish to utilize it.

Say you're willing to accept a 7% rate of return. Here's the formula:

$$\text{Value} = \frac{\$3,000}{7\%}$$

The value of the property is now $42,857, or the most you can pay in order to receive the 7% rate of return you desire.

Appraisers shouldn't perform income capitalization appraisal because the appraiser won't know the rate of return you want. The appraiser can perform a cost approach appraisal to provide a different view of the property's value, but if you're investing for income, the income capitalization approach is the only way to be sure you'll get the rate of return you seek.

Lenders use appraisals to make sure they don't loan more than the property is worth. Buyers use appraisals to make sure they don't overpay for a property, and sellers use appraisals to help them properly value their properties for sale.

Let the appraiser develop an unbiased appraisal rather than targeting the appraisal to some predetermined value. Many forms of real estate and mortgage fraud rely on inflated appraisals, so the fraudster can obtain a mortgage loan for more than the property is worth and use the excess money for other purposes. Keep in mind that this practice is illegal, unethical, and harmful to homeowners, neighborhoods, and the local economy (and even the state, national, and global economy, when it gets out of hand).

MYTH # **70**

I Can Trust What the Homeowners Tell Me.

Fact: They May Not Lie to You, but That Doesn't Mean Their Comments Are Accurate

Homeowners facing foreclosure have no reason, legal or otherwise, to share any information with you. They're also emotionally fragile due to the circumstances they find themselves in.

Some homeowners are so desperate they'll do anything they can to convince you to let them stay in the home or to pay them at or above market value. Homeowners have told us the house is in perfect condition, they have money coming in soon and will catch up on all payments, they'll move out in a week or so as soon as they find a place to live, or they'll play on our emotions and claim that someone close to them is ill or has recently passed away. Ralph even had a couple tell him their baby had died. (Their baby hadn't died.) Confirm or question any claim or excuse that sounds fishy or odd.

If you take a step back and consider the situation objectively, it's understandable for homeowners to bend the truth. They're in a desperate situation and are not only facing the loss of the biggest purchase and investment they've ever made, but also the loss of a place where they've created family memories. As an investor, you should be compassionate, but don't be gullible. Offer a suitable concession if you feel it's appropriate, have the homeowners agree to that concession in writing, and then hold them to their agreements.

Other claims you can easily verify. If a homeowner claims the house is in great shape, simply say, "Great—then the inspection will be a breeze." If they object to an inspection, that should raise a red flag.

Record any conversations you have with homeowners. Ask the homeowners, for their protection and yours, whether they will allow you to record your conversations. (Make sure you record yourself asking their permission and them giving permission.) By recording your conversations, you have an audio record of exactly what you told the homeowners and what they told you, should disagreements ever arise as to what has been said.

MYTH # **71**

If I Find Myself in Financial Difficulty, I'll Never Escape Foreclosure.

Fact: There Are a Number of Ways You Can Stave off Disaster

Not only can understanding how to dig out of a financial hole help you, but it can also help you advise a homeowner facing the same crisis.

Let's recap a little. If you are one month behind on your mortgage payments, you're delinquent, but you're not in danger of foreclosure. If you are two months behind, by law the lender can initiate foreclosure proceedings. In either case, the lender calls and sends you letters warning you that you face foreclosure, even if they do not actually initiate the process at that time.

If the reason you're in mortgage distress is due to a short-term problem, such as a medical situation or an emergency, that required unusual spending, then negotiating a simple payment plan with your lender to bring your mortgage back to a current status may be all that's required. If the problem is more serious, you may need to negotiate a more complicated plan and possibly take other steps to save your home.

Either way, you'll have to present information to the lender to show why you're in mortgage distress and, more importantly, how you'll bring your mortgage back to a current status so you can keep your home.

Here is a summary of the basic steps you should take.

Gather and Retain Information. Keep track of pertinent details: Your account number, the address and phone number of your lender, and any other information about your mortgage. Write down the date and time of all calls, whom you speak to, what their title is, what they say, and what you say or agree to during the call. Record all calls and correspondence you receive from the lender or anyone else connected with your mortgage.

Don't forget to write down messages left for you on your answering machine. Each is an attempt to reach you; the lender will be documenting those attempts, so you should document them as well. Avoiding answering the phone or opening your mail will not delay the foreclosure process.

Your goal is to stay organized, stay on top of correspondence, and always act in a professional manner. Your credibility will be taken into account by the lender as you negotiate, and the more professional you come across, the better your chances of successfully negotiating with the lender.

Remember that lenders want you to keep your home. They make money from the interest on your loans, but they very rarely make money on foreclosures. That doesn't mean they *won't* foreclose, but it's not the lender's first choice.

Evaluate Why You Face Foreclosure. You will need to properly respond to questions when you communicate with the lender. While you may have a number of excuses for why you fell behind, there are only three basic reasons for defaulting on a mortgage agreement:

1. A reduction in family income
2. Unexpected expenses: medical bills, emergencies, and so on.
3. Lack of control over expenses due to personal choices that you have made

The lender will want to know why you're behind. Be prepared to explain. You should also not be tempted to shade the truth. Be honest with the lender. If the lender has reason to feel you are being dishonest or unethical, it has no reason to think you'll uphold any agreement you make to save your home.

Evaluate Your Income and Expenses. Write down your monthly income after taxes and without overtime. Below that, list all expenses. Make sure you list everything. Put your mortgage payment at the top of the list, followed by anything else you and your family spends, whether on bills, entertainment, food, utilities, or other items.

Do not leave out any expense no matter how insignificant. When you present your plan to your lender, the lender will sense-check your plan, and if you haven't accounted for basic expenses like food or utility costs, the lender will know your plan is unrealistic and will not accept it. You haven't developed a workable plan if it doesn't reflect the reality of your situation.

Determine How to Bring Your Mortgage Current. In order to keep your home, your mortgage payment must be your first priority. Plan to pay it in full before any other bill is paid or expense is incurred. That may sound harsh, but think about it this way: Does it do any good to have a new couch when you are about to lose your home?

Talk to your family. Agree to cut out entertainment, delay purchases, and find any way possible to cut costs until you get caught up on your bills, especially your mortgage. The only way to avoid the threat of foreclosure, or of any credit-related problems, is to consistently live within your means.

Now assess your income and your expenses. Subtract all your expenses from your monthly take-home pay. If you have more expenses than money available, you are overextended. Your mortgage difficulties aren't due to a short-term problem; they're a sign of a long-term financial crisis. You'll need to free up money immediately to make your mortgage payments.

To buy yourself time, let your other creditors know, in writing, that you are headed toward foreclosure. Ask whether they are willing to set up a reduced-payment plan rather than have you completely default on them or even file bankruptcy.

If your take-home pay is more than expenses, you should be able to cover all your bills and keep your mortgage current. If you are not paying your mortgage on time, then you do not have control over your expenses.

Set up a budget and stick to it. Look at your expenses and cut out anything that is unnecessary or place it in its proper priority, which is after the mortgage payment.

We realize there are emergencies and even personal-crisis situations that you can't foresee, but take the time to weigh everything. Don't act emotionally and then suffer for hasty decisions later. Write out a plan to get back on track with your mortgage if you have faced a major financial burden beyond your control.

To make sure you stick with your budget, end all credit card purchases immediately. Even consider trading in a car you are making large monthly payments on for one you can pay for in full that will cost you less in monthly payments and insurance premiums. Then consider whether you can borrow from resources like insurance policies, thrift savings plan, or 401(k) or IRA accounts.

Lenders will be more inclined to work with you when you can show, in writing, everything you have tried to bring your mortgage current. Make sure you keep detailed records so you can prove to your lender how serious you are about solving your financial problems and bringing your mortgage back to a current status.

If these steps haven't solved your problem, there are still other options. Aside from selling the home (which may still be your best option), you can try to modify your original mortgage terms or create a forbearance plan.

- **Modification of mortgage terms:** If the lender agrees, you can change your original mortgage agreement in regard to the due date or interest rate, or by increasing your principal balance by adding the amount of money you're behind to your outstanding balance. If the lender agrees, the basic terms of your mortgage change, and you make monthly payments based on your new mortgage terms.
- **Forbearance plan:** A forbearance plan allows you catch up on back payments over time (usually up to 18 months). Let's say you're three months behind on your payments. The lender can agree for you to make a payment and a half until you catch up instead of requiring the full amount be paid at one time. For instance, if your monthly payment is $800 and you're three months behind, you'll need to pay

$2,400 to bring your mortgage current. If the lender agrees, you could make monthly payments of $1,100 for eight months, bringing your mortgage current at the end of that eight-month period. You'll have made your normal payments of $800 per month and eight payments of an additional $300 per month to satisfy the $2,400 in monthly payments you're behind. If you can document your income and expenses, and the lender is confident in your ability to pay, the lender may agree to forbearance.

Now let's talk briefly about contacting the lender. If possible, try to call your lender before your lender calls you. You will have already received letters, but at some point a representative will call you. If you call first, you'll improve your credibility, since you're being proactive by contacting the lender to work out a solution. Most homeowners don't make the first call.

The lender will ask you why you fell behind and when it can expect payment in full. The lender will also possibly ask what your monthly expenses are, especially if it is willing to work out a plan or an arrangement. Different lenders have different policies.

Keep your notes close by to refer to when you speak to the lender. Don't respond to questions without facts to back you up.

Remember that the lender will document what you say. For that reason alone it is better to answer a question truthfully, or even to say, "I am not sure, but I will call you back," than to make up an answer. (If you say you will call back, be sure to call back.)

As we've mentioned a number of times, the lender doesn't want to foreclose, so make sure you work hard to show the representative a plan the lender can accept that will let you bring your mortgage current.

Most people facing foreclosure mistakenly believe that they have only two options: Pay up or move out. They actually have about a dozen options, including selling the home (to pay off the mortgage balance and walk away with any remaining equity), selling to an investor, reinstating the loan (by catching up on missed payments), forbearance, mortgage modification, abandoning the home (if your credit is already damaged and you owe more on the house than you can sell it for), and deed in lieu of foreclosure (handing the property over to the lender in exchange for the lender forgiving your debt). If you are facing foreclosure, don't panic. Explore all of your options, and choose the one that's most appealing.

MYTH # **72**

I'll Be Able to Flip This House in a Couple of Weeks!

Fact: Congratulations if You Do, but Your Chances Are Slim

First, a definition: Most investors define *flipping* to mean the process of purchasing an undervalued and/or poorly maintained house, making repairs and renovations as quickly as possible to bring the house up to neighborhood standards, and selling for a profit.

You may be able to sell a property to another investor the very same day you complete the purchase, but obviously you will have had no time to make repairs or renovations. In that case, your goal is to make a reasonable profit.

Unless you're wholesaling properties, assuming foreclosure investing is a way to generate quick cash and quick profits is a mistake. Allow time for delays, unexpected renovations, and a slow sale, especially if the market cools off in your area. If you analyze a deal and the only way to make a reasonable profit is to flip the property in less than a month, your risk in all likelihood outweighs the reward. Either find another investor to quickly sell the property to or find a better opportunity.

In addition to the normal time it takes to rehab a property, list it, and sell it, purchasing properties in pre-foreclosure or at an auction can have other types of delays, including the following:

- ◆ Homeowners can take time to make and rethink their decisions.
- ◆ Courts or trustees can delay the process.

- Homeowners can change their minds at the last minute.
- Redemption periods can last up to a year.

You can expect to pay about $100 per day in holding costs. That represents about $3,000 per month. Be sure to include these costs in your calculations. If the redemption period is six months in your area, can you afford to pay $18,000 in holding costs and still profit from the property? Do the math, and if the deal doesn't make sense, don't do the deal.

 Always account for *at least* two months of holding costs. Even if you perform a minor miracle and can have the house ready to place on the market in two weeks, the home will take at least four to six weeks to sell under normal market conditions. If the market is slow, the average amount of time to sell a home can be six months or more. Keep your finger on the pulse of the ever-changing housing market and calculate your costs accordingly, but never figure on holding a property for fewer than two months.

MYTH # **73**

If I Make Some Repairs Before I Take Possession of the Property, I'll Save Valuable Time.

Fact: Time Saved Could Turn into Money Down the Drain

Investors often become overly enthusiastic. They purchase a home at a foreclosure auction and figure they can get an early start on repairs and renovations during the redemption period. They may even convince the homeowner to let them start on repairs and renovations before they've moved out. This might seem like a good idea. After all, if you are buying foreclosures in an area with a six-month redemption period, holding costs can be quite steep. Why not do everything possible to have the house ready as soon as the redemption period ends?

That's not such a good idea, because the homeowners or another investor may step in and buy the property back from you, meaning that whatever repairs and renovations you made become a free gift to the new happy homeowners. If you think this can never happen, think again. It has happened, and the overly enthusiastic investors got seriously burned.

During the redemption period, you own what is called a *nonperforming investment*: The investment does not earn any return. You will profit only when you sell the property or rent it to others, and you cannot do either until the redemption period is complete. If the property needs repairs or preventive maintenance that will prevent costlier repairs down the road, make those repairs if the property is vacant or the homeowners give you permission. But hedge your investment: If the roof is leaking, instead of replacing the entire roof, make basic repairs that will take care of the problem for the time being. A $1,000 repair job will limit the water damage caused to the interior of the home and will help you avoid the expense (for now, at least) of replacing the entire roof.

Even though you don't own the property, you can plan your renovations and line up contractors. When the redemption period is over, you can hit the ground running and complete your work as quickly as possible. But don't start renovations early, or you may lose all the time and money you invest.

If you live in an area in which homeowners have redemption rights, study the redemption rules carefully; they can be quite complex. In Michigan, for example, the redemption period for most homeowners is six months, but if the home is on a parcel of land larger than three acres, the redemption period is 12 months. Ralph's team once worked on a case in which the homeowners were soon going to be kicked out of their home, because their redemption period was ready to expire. While examining the paperwork, they noticed that the couple owned five acres. The bank had made a critical mistake. Ralph's team turned the matter over to an attorney representing the couple, and the attorney was able to convince the courts to restart the redemption clock. Now the couple had an additional 12 months to find new employment and catch up on their payments! Ralph's team lost the property, but they made friends for life.

MYTH # **74**

It's a Stretch, but I Think I Can Make an Extra $10,000 on This Property.

Fact: Don't Be Greedy; If Your Return Justifies the Risk, You've Done Very Well

Your first goal is to purchase any foreclosure property for significantly below market value. Your second goal is to repair and renovate the property as quickly as possible before holding costs gobble up your profits. Your goal is not to spend so much on the property that you price it out of range for buyers in that area. Trying to make excessive profits frequently backfires: For every deal where you manage to squeeze an extra $5,000 in profits, you'll have five deals where those same efforts cause your house to sit on the market for months.

What should you do? Aim to make a good profit and move on to the next profitable deal.

Before you purchase any property, you should develop a plan for renovations and repairs. Not only will your plan keep your spending on track, it will also create a timeline to ensure you complete renovations as quickly as possible. Basic strategies fall into these four main categories:

1. **No renovations:** Buy a property and quickly sell it to another investor. Many investors find bargains and simply resell them, aiming for a $10,000 to $20,000 profit on each transaction.
2. **Quick cosmetics:** Find a house in good repair but in need of a thorough cleaning. Clean everything, take care of minor defects, repair all the systems (air conditioning, furnace, electrical systems, plumbing), and paint the walls and ceilings white. Price the house below market value, so it will sell quickly. Many buyers love the chance to perform other cosmetic changes to suit their tastes.
3. **Complete rehab:** Clean the house, paint the walls white, and perform extensive cosmetic changes like new carpeting throughout. Also focus on bringing the kitchen and bathrooms up to date, since those are the rooms buyers will focus on most.

4. **Renovations that add value:** After you've performed a complete rehab, add a new feature or features to the house: A new deck, a bedroom addition, central heating and air conditioning, or an extra bathroom may boost the property into a higher price bracket. Your goal is to bring a house up to the standard of the neighborhood; if most of the nearby houses have two bathrooms, adding a bathroom to a one-bath foreclosure property will yield real returns. Adding a fourth bathroom to a house in a neighborhood filled with 1.5-bath homes likely will not.

Remember, your goal is to spend wisely and bring the property up to the market standard in its neighborhood. No matter what renovations you make, buyers will almost never pay $300,000 for a property in a neighborhood where the next-best house sells for $250,000. Why take the risk?

In some cases, you may be able to add real value to the home. Converting an attic into an extra bedroom or finishing a basement can be relatively inexpensive ways to add value. The key is to determine whether these value-added renovations are worth the time and money you'll spend. To determine whether a feature you're considering is worth the expense:

- **Check comparables.** Determine the value of comparable properties with the feature you're considering. If you plan to add a fourth bedroom, check the recent sales prices of four-bedroom homes against the sales prices of three-bedroom homes (all other features considered equal, of course). If you have to spend $10,000 adding a fourth bedroom that will bring an $11,000 return, the reward does not outweigh the risk.
- **Assess local demand:** Visit open houses and talk to your real estate agent to learn what local buyers are looking for. Your goal is to make your house attractive to buyers interested in the neighborhood. Find out how much extra buyers are willing to spend for the features your house is missing.
- **Weigh the cost.** No matter what the return, some renovations will be outside your range. If you have a total of $10,000 budgeted for

renovations, considering a $20,000 kitchen makeover is obviously a waste of time. Consider other renovations or, if the expected return is high enough, consider borrowing additional funds.

Some investors actively seek properties with missing features; they pay below market prices for the properties, add the missing feature to bring the property in line with other homes in the area, and sell for handsome profits.

Here are some ideas for improvements you can make to add real value to the home:

- ◆ Add a deck or patio.
- ◆ Convert unused or unfinished space into living space.
- ◆ Add a bathroom.
- ◆ Add a bedroom.
- ◆ Add a garage.
- ◆ Replace windows.
- ◆ Replace doors.
- ◆ Add central air conditioning (if not present).
- ◆ Open up the floor plan by converting two small rooms into one larger room.

You can take the same approach, but don't try to make a killing on each transaction. Make a fair profit while reducing your holding costs by getting in and out quickly.

You want to offer buyers the best property in its class at the best price, so it will sell in a hurry and earn a reasonable profit. Offering the best property in its class at the best price means rehabbing the property to bring it in line or making it slightly more attractive than other properties currently on the market in the same price range, but not improving the property so much that you have to jack up the price or wipe out your profit. If 10 comparable homes are for sale in your area, you want your home to be one of the top 2 or 3.

MYTH # **75**

I'm Making Good Money on Real Estate, but I Should Keep My Day Job.

Fact: Focus on Your Greatest Return and What You Enjoy Doing Most

Let's say you're an accountant working for a large corporation. You make $65,000 per year. Why did you choose the job you have? Hopefully it's because you enjoy the work and you feel the pay and benefits are appropriate for your talents, background, and experience. (If that's not the case, can we assume you're actively seeking another job?)

Now say you have been investing in foreclosure properties in your spare time. Over the last three years, you've bought and sold four properties per year for an average profit of $20,000. You have grown confident in your ability to spot good opportunities, make cost-effective repairs and renovations, and make a reasonable profit. You've also found good people to work with: your lender, real estate agent, title company, attorney, and a few key contractors you can count on. Should you keep your full-time job or take the plunge and become a full-time real estate investor?

What do you enjoy doing the most? If you enjoy real estate investing and feel you can replace your full-time income by handling three or four more foreclosures each year, why wouldn't you? If you feel you could put more total money in your pocket by handling five or six more foreclosures (and again, you enjoy the work), so much the better.

Would you take a higher-paying accounting job? Our guess is yes. If you enjoy real estate investing and you can earn more, why not?

At the same time, everyone's path is different. Some investors enjoy doing two or three real estate deals a year; taking on any more would create too much pressure and too many demands on their time. Others like the security of keeping a full-time job; in their case, security is more important than the potential for higher income.

Each of us must decide what is most important and act accordingly. Choose the path that's right for you and follow it. The last thing any of us wants to do is to look back and wish we had chosen a different path.

When you're trying to decide whether to take the leap and become a full-time real estate investor, don't forget to account for any additional benefits you may be receiving with your full-time job, including health insurance, paid vacations, retirement, and health insurance. All those things taken together can represent a good chunk of change.

MYTH # **76**

I've Put So Much Time into This Deal—I Refuse to Let Anyone Outbid Me!

Fact: You May Be Attached to the Deal, but the Deal Is Not Attached to You

A friend of ours owns a 1965 Ford Mustang. The previous owner had stored it in his backyard (don't ask). Our friend spent years and hundreds of hours painstakingly restoring the entire car to its original condition. It is a beautiful car, and is probably worth between $40,000 and $50,000.

The problem is that our friend is convinced the car is worth at least $100,000, not because that's a realistic market value, but because he spent so much time and effort on the car. He loves the car, but the car doesn't love him back.

The same applies to real estate investing. No matter how much time you spend evaluating a deal, talking with homeowners, working through issues with other lien holders, and planning renovations and repairs, in the end your only concern should be whether you can make a reasonable profit on the transaction. If you can't, it doesn't matter how much time you spent—it's not a good deal.

We discussed buyer's panic in Myth #52. Panic can set in when you think a deal is too good to be true and you don't want it to slip away, but you can also panic when you see all your hard work going down the drain as the bidding rises above your walk-away price. Don't panic: Stick to your guns and walk away.

Good investors are rational and objective, and most of all they check their emotions at the doorstep. Be professional, be courteous, and be considerate, but don't get emotional. Your "wins" and "losses" are determined when you calculate your profits after you sell a property, not at the auction.

It can also be tempting to become emotional dealing with homeowners in pre-foreclosure. Although we do encourage you to empathize with homeowners who are under duress, don't go too far in sympathizing with them. Lifeguards are careful to remember that drowning people can take them under, too. You want to save the homeowners from experiencing any more pain without having them take you under. Inform them of their options, offer them a fair deal, but don't give away all of your profits trying to help them. Always keep in mind that this is a business deal, and good deals benefit *both* parties, which includes you.

MYTH # **77**

Foreclosure Investing Is Just Too Complicated—I Can't Do It.

Fact: You Absolutely Can—and Other Professionals Will Help You

The first time you call a homeowner in pre-foreclosure you'll be nervous. The first time you attend a foreclosure auction with a cashier's check in your pocket, you'll feel the stress. If you're the high bidder, you'll be excited but also a little scared.

Don't let these feelings bother you. All successful investors were nervous and even a little scared when they bought their first foreclosure. It's natural: You're taking a risk. Foreclosure investing involves a certain degree of risk—that's why the returns can be high. Your goal as a smart investor is to reduce your risk by building a good team, thoroughly evaluating properties, using your eyes before you buy, anticipating and preparing for surprises by developing contingencies, and most of all being willing to work hard to overcome obstacles or roadblocks. But no matter how hard you try, some amount of risk is always involved, so it's okay to be nervous.

Taking on new challenges can be stressful and scary. Don't let those emotions cause you to decide foreclosure investing is too complicated, because it's not. The rules and regulations governing foreclosures are straightforward and understandable, although the learning curve can be a little steep at first. Foreclosure is simply a *process,* and any process can be learned. Real estate investors come from all walks of life and all educational backgrounds.

A built-in safety net also exists, right where you live. Real estate professionals are in business to help people just like you. Real estate agents need you; they need homes to sell or they don't earn commissions. Lenders need you. Contractors need you. Title companies need you. Attorneys need you. Good real estate professionals will welcome your calls and your questions. You hope to build long-term business relationships, and so do they.

Successful foreclosure investing takes time and experience. More importantly, it takes motivation, drive, determination, and hard work. You can overcome inexperience by doing your homework, asking for guidance, and working hard.

Stick with it and soon you'll be experienced—and, we hope, willing to pass on some of the wisdom you've gained to others who can benefit from the path you've chosen.

Good luck and happy investing!

Planes are much safer on the runway than they are in flight, but eventually, to make the best use of an airplane, it has to take off. Being fearful and hesitant is healthy at first. Remember how you felt when you first started driving? Eventually, with a little practice, investing in foreclosures can become as second-nature as driving a car. Keep at it; keep practicing. It will get easier, but you still need to do your homework and keep your eyes on the road.

Appendix

Resources

When searching for good foreclosure properties and structuring your deals, the following resources will provide a great deal of assistance:

Foreclosure Properties and Statistics

www.RealtyTrac.com

www.hud.gov/homes/homesforsale.cfm—HUD (Housing and Urban Development) homes for sale

www.foreclosurefreesearch.com

www.homesales.gov—Homes for sale by the U.S. government

www.treas.gov/auctions/irs—Internal Revenue Service auctions

www.fdic.gov/buying/index.html—Federal Deposit Insurance Corporation

www.sba.gov/assets.html—Small Business Administration

www.ocwen.com—Ocwen

www.treas.gov/auctions/customs/realprop.html—U.S. Customs Seizures

www.resales.usda.gov—USDA Real Estate for Sale

In addition, many lenders and banks have individual pages listing REO properties for sale.

Approximate Property Values

www.Zillow.com

www.HouseValues.com

www.Intelius.com

http://realestate.yahoo.com/Homevalues

www.RealEstateabc.com

Warning: Don't place too much stock in these online real estate valuation sites. Local real estate agents and appraisers are still the best source of current local market conditions and values.

Documentation and Regulatory Guidance and Other Resource Sites

www.MBAA.org

www.MortgageMyths.com—Mortgage information

www.GetFlipping.com—Property-flipping and foreclosure and pre-foreclosure investing information

www.ForeclosureSelfDefense.com—Information for homeowners facing foreclosure

www.Realtor.com—Search for qualified Realtors®

www.NAMB.org—Search for qualified mortgage brokers

Check individual state web sites for current foreclosure guidelines that are state specific.

Books

Foreclosure Investing For Dummies by Ralph R. Roberts with Joe Kraynak (John Wiley & Sons)

Foreclosure Self-Defense For Dummies by Ralph R. Roberts, Lois Maljak, and Paul Doroh, with Joe Kraynak (John Wiley & Sons)

Mortgage Myths: 77 Secrets That Will Save You Thousands on Home Financing by Chip Cummings and Ralph R. Roberts (John Wiley & Sons)

Sample Forms and Checklists

Here are several checklists and worksheets to assist you in evaluating foreclosure properties. In addition, you can download all of these forms electronically from www.TheForeclosureMyths.com.

Walk-Away Calculation Worksheet

Property Address: _____ Date Prepared: _____

Estimated Value (*after improvements*) $ _____
Adjusted Market Value*   /□ 1.20   □ 1.25   □ 1.30   = **$** _____

Closing Costs (*at purchase*) $ _____
Holding Costs $ _____× _____ months $ _____
Repairs $ _____
Back Taxes (*if any*) $ _____
Contingency Fund $ _____
Total Expenses   −$ _____

Real Estate Commissions $ _____
Closing Costs (*at sale*) $ _____
Total Costs of Sale   −$ _____

Walk-Away Price   =$ _____

**For rising property values, use 1.20; steady, 1.25; declining, 1.30; divide Estimated Value by factor to arrive at Adjusted Market Value.*

Property Inspection Checklist

Inspection Date _____

Property Address _____ ☐ Exterior Only
City, County, State _____ ☐ Interior/Exterior
Owner/Contact _____ Phone _____
Sq. Ft: _____ B/R: _____ Bath: _____ Stories: _____ Lot: _____
Other:_____

Location/Area

Comments

Neighborhood	G	F	P	
Schools	G	F	P	
Access to shopping	G	F	P	
Streets/highway access	G	F	P	
Home fits in with surrounding properties	G	F	P	

Exterior

	Condition*			Repair Cost
General structure of building	G	F	P	$_____
Siding	G	F	P	$_____
Roof	G	F	P	$_____
Garage	G	F	P	$_____
Landscaping	G	F	P	$_____
Windows	G	F	P	$_____
Paint/trim	G	F	P	$_____
Outbuildings	G	F	P	$_____
Central A/C visible	G	F	P	$_____
Pool	G	F	P	$_____

Interior — Condition* — Repair Cost

Interior	Condition*			Repair Cost
Kitchen—counters, cabinets, etc.	G	F	P	$ _____
Appliances	G	F	P	$ _____
Bathrooms—toilet, fixtures, shower, etc.	G	F	P	$ _____
Plumbing	G	F	P	$ _____
Electrical	G	F	P	$ _____
Furnace/cooling	G	F	P	$ _____
Water heater	G	F	P	$ _____
Basement	G	F	P	$ _____
Carpet	G	F	P	$ _____
Doors/windows/walls	G	F	P	$ _____
Paint	G	F	P	$ _____
Attic/crawlspace	G	F	P	$ _____

TOTAL COST OF REPAIRS: $ _____

*Good; Fair; Poor.

Foreclosure Auction Data Sheet

Sale Date _____

Property Address _____ Time _____

City, Country, State_____ Location _____

Owner/Contact _____ Phone _____

Opening Bid: $_____ Walk-Away Bid: $_____

☐ **Pre-bid package required**

First mortgage: $ _____

Junior liens: $ _____

Costs/fees: $ _____

Taxes: $ _____

Special assessments: $ _____

Sale Notice
(paste here)

☐ **Previously on market**

List price: $ _____

Realtor: _____

Phone: _____

Number of bidders present: _____

Winning bid: $ _____

☐ **Lien holder bid**

☐ **Bid accepted**

Chk #_____

Purchase amount: $ _____

Down payment made: $ _____

Balance: $ _____

Due on: _____

State Foreclosure Guidelines

It is important to understand the rules for the jurisdiction and state where the property is located prior to pursuing the foreclosure market. We have listed the current rules and regulations for all 50 states and Washington D.C. Here is a guide to the listing information:

- **Type of foreclosure process:** This can be *judicial* or *nonjudicial*, or even both! A judicial process involves a lawsuit by the lender, and is handled by the Court. A nonjudicial process is involved when there is a preauthorized "power of sale" in the mortgage document or Deed of Trust. This allows the lender to foreclose directly to pay off the loan balance and any costs.
- **Process period:** This is the average amount of time it takes for the foreclosure to go from the initial foreclosure notice (or notice of default) to the time possession is transferred to a new owner.
- **Type of deed:** The type of deed involved can be a *Mortgage Deed*, a *Deed of Trust*, or both. A Mortgage Deed is a specific contract between the borrower and lender that allows the lender to foreclose in event of default. A Deed of Trust is a contract that puts control of the deed with a trustee—a neutral third party. In this case, the trustee forecloses when the borrower defaults on the loan.
- **Notice of default (NOD):** Some states require that a NOD be sent to the borrowers informing them of their default status on the loan.
- **Notice of sale requirements:** This is a published and posted notice indicating the specific date, time, place, and terms of a foreclosure sale. It will include the property address and legal description as well as borrower and lender information. It may be overridden by mortgage documents.
- **Redemption period requirements:** A period of time after the sale in which the foreclosed borrower has the right to redeem the property by paying off the loan and all costs—including attorney fees, penalties, and interest.

The following information is considered to be up-to-date and accurate as of time of publication, but as with everything, things do change. These rules and regulations can also sometimes vary from county to county, so consult the county clerk or register of deeds or a qualified real estate attorney for any clarification or additional details. Double-check the information presented here against information provided on state and county web sites.

Alabama

Type of foreclosure process: Both; nonjudicial is more common.
Process period: 60 to 90 days average.
Type of deed: Both are used.
Notice of default: Not state mandated, but may be included in lender documents.
Notice of sale requirements: Posted at courthouse and 3 other public places; 3 weeks' notice in local newspaper and as directed by individual mortgage document.
Redemption period requirements: 12 months.

Alaska

Type of foreclosure process: Both; nonjudicial is more common.
Process period: 90 days average.
Type of deed: Both are used.
Notice of default: Varies by area.
Notice of sale requirements: Notice in local newspaper for 4 consecutive weeks and in 3 public places, one of which has to be closest U.S. Postal office, 30 days prior to the date of sale.
Redemption period requirements: 12 months for judicial; none for nonjudicial.

Arizona

Type of foreclosure process: Nonjudicial.
Process period: 90 days.
Type of deed: Both.
Notice of default: None.
Notice of sale requirements: Notice must be published in local newspaper for 4 consecutive weeks, with last notice appearing no less

than 10 days prior to sale; mailed to all lien holders and borrower at least 3 months prior to sale; posted at courthouse and on property at least 20 days prior to sale.

Redemption period requirements: None.

Arkansas

Type of foreclosure process: Both.

Process period: 90 to 120 days average.

Type of deed: Both.

Notice of default: Must be filed with county and mailed to borrower (nonjudicial).

Notice of sale requirements: 4 consecutive weeks listed in local newspaper; final notice must appear at least 10 days prior to the sale; posted in the county recorder's office.

Redemption period requirements: 12 months for judicial; none for nonjudicial.

California

Type of foreclosure process: Both; nonjudicial is more common.

Process period: 120 days.

Type of deed: Both.

Notice of default: Notice must be filed with county and mailed to all borrowers and lien holders.

Notice of sale requirements: Published in local newspaper for 3 consecutive weeks at least 20 days prior to sale; recorded with county at least 14 days prior to sale; posted on property and in at least 1 public location a minimum of 20 days prior to sale.

Redemption period requirements: 365 days for judicial; none for nonjudicial.

Colorado

Type of foreclosure process: Both; nonjudicial is more common.

Process period: 45 to 180 days average.

Type of deed: Deed of Trust.

Notice of default: None.

Notice of sale requirements: Mailed to borrower and published 5 weeks in local newspaper.

Redemption period requirements: 75 days for residential; 180 days for agricultural.

Connecticut

Type of foreclosure process: Judicial.

Process period: 60 to 150 days average.

Type of deed: Mortgage Deed.

Notice of default: None.

Notice of sale requirements: Notice published by attorney.

Redemption period requirements: Decided by court.

Delaware

Type of foreclosure process: Judicial.

Process period: 210 to 300 days.

Type of deed: Mortgage Deed.

Notice of default: None.

Notice of sale requirements: Notice to borrower at least 10 days prior to sale; 14 days posting on the property; published in two local newspapers no more than 3 times per week for 2 weeks prior to sale.

Redemption period requirements: None; borrower may contest sale prior to court confirmation.

Florida

Type of foreclosure process: Judicial.

Process period: 150 to 180 days average.

Type of deed: Mortgage Deed.

Notice of default: None required.

Notice of sale requirements: Notice to be published in local newspaper for 2 consecutive weeks prior to sale; second notice to be at least 5 days prior to sale.

Redemption period requirements: None.

Georgia

Type of foreclosure process: Both; nonjudicial is more common.

Process period: 60 to 90 days average.

Type of deed: Both.

Notice of default: None required.

Notice of sale requirements: Notice to borrower at least 15 days prior to sale; publication in local newspaper for 4 weeks prior to sale.

Redemption period requirements: None.

Hawaii

Type of foreclosure process: Both.

Process period: 180 days nonjudicial; 330 days judicial.

Type of deed: Both.

Notice of default: As required by mortgage clause.

Notice of sale requirements: Notice to borrower at least 21 days before sale; publication in local newspaper for 3 consecutive weeks prior to sale, with final notice appearing at least 14 days prior to sale.

Redemption period requirements: None.

Idaho

Type of foreclosure process: Both; nonjudicial is more common.

Process period: 150 to 180 days for nonjudicial; 330 days for judicial.

Type of deed: Both.

Notice of default: Notice to be mailed to borrower and lien holders or interested parties as filed with county recorder's office.

Notice of sale requirements: Notice mailed to borrower 120 days prior to sale; publication in local newspaper for 4 consecutive weeks, with final notice to appear not less than 30 days prior to sale.

Redemption period requirements: 365 days judicial; none for nonjudicial.

Illinois

Type of foreclosure process: Judicial.

Process period: 300 to 360 days average.

Type of deed: Mortgage Deed.

Notice of default: None.

Notice of sale requirements: Notice sent to borrower and all lien holders; published in local newspaper for 3 consecutive weeks no more than 45 days prior to sale, with last notice appearing no less than 7 days prior to sale.

Redemption period requirements: 90 days.

Indiana

Type of foreclosure process: Judicial.

Process period: 150 to 270 days average.

Type of deed: Mortgage Deed.

Notice of default: None.

Notice of sale requirements: Personal delivery by sheriff to borrower; notice published in local newspaper for 3 consecutive weeks no more than 30 days prior to sale; posted in at least 3 public places and in county courthouse.

Redemption period requirements: None.

Iowa

Type of foreclosure process: Both; nonjudicial by request.

Process period: 120 to 180 days average.

Type of deed: Mortgage Deed.

Notice of default: Notice required to borrower.

Notice of sale requirements: Notice delivered to borrower at least 20 days prior to sale; publication in local newspaper with first notice at least 4 weeks prior to sale and again 2 weeks prior to sale; posted in three public places including county courthouse.

Redemption period requirements: Variable.

Kansas

Type of foreclosure process: Judicial.

Process period: 12 to 24 months.

Type of deed: Mortgage Deed.

Notice of default: Required to borrower.

Notice of sale requirements: Notice to be published in local newspaper for 3 consecutive weeks prior to sale.

Redemption period requirements: 90 days if vacant; 180 days if occupied.

Kentucky
Type of foreclosure process: Judicial.

Process period: 180 days.

Type of deed: Mortgage Deed

Notice of default: None.

Notice of sale requirements: Published in local newspaper for 3 consecutive weeks prior to sale.

Redemption period requirements: 12 months.

Louisiana
Type of foreclosure process: Judicial.

Process period: 60 to 270 days (shorter is typical).

Type of deed: Mortgage Deed.

Notice of default: None.

Notice of sale requirements: Personal service by sheriff to borrower; publication in a local newspaper twice prior to sale for a minimum of 30 days.

Redemption period requirements: None.

Maine
Type of foreclosure process: Judicial.

Process period: 180 to 210 days average.

Type of deed: Mortgage Deed.

Notice of default: Notice required to be served to borrower prior to sale.

Notice of sale requirements: Published in local newspaper 3 weeks prior to sale.

Redemption period requirements: 90 days.

Maryland
Type of foreclosure process: Judicial.

Process period: 60 to 90 days average.

Type of deed: Both.

Notice of default: None.

Notice of sale requirements: Notice to borrower and all lien holders at least 10 days prior to sale; publication in local newspaper 3 weeks prior to sale.

Redemption period requirements: Court mandates.

Massachusetts

Type of foreclosure process: Both.

Process period: 75 to 90 days.

Type of deed: Both.

Notice of default: None.

Notice of sale requirements: Notice to borrower and all lien holders at least 14 days prior to sale; publication in local newspaper 3 consecutive weeks prior to sale, with first notice no less than 21 days prior.

Redemption period requirements: None.

Michigan

Type of foreclosure process: Both.

Process period: 90 to 420 days.

Type of deed: Both.

Notice of default: None.

Notice of sale requirements: Publication in local newspaper for 4 consecutive weeks prior to sale, with first notice at least 28 days prior. Posting on property for same period.

Redemption period requirements: 180 to 365 days; 30 days if vacant.

Minnesota

Type of foreclosure process: Both; mostly nonjudicial.

Process period: 120 days.

Type of deed: Both.

Notice of default: Required to borrower.

Notice of sale requirements: Personal service to borrower at least 4 weeks prior to sale; publication in local newspaper for 6 weeks prior to sale.

Redemption period requirements: 6 to 12 months.

Mississippi

Type of foreclosure process: Both; mostly nonjudicial.

Process period: 90 to 120 days.

Type of deed: Both.

Notice of default: 30 days prior to sale.

Notice of sale requirements: Notice posted at county courthouse; published in local newspaper for 3 weeks prior to sale.

Redemption period requirements: None.

Missouri

Type of foreclosure process: Both; mostly nonjudicial.

Process period: 21 to 45 days.

Type of deed: Both.

Notice of default: Required to borrower.

Notice of sale requirements: Notice to borrower and lien holders at least 20 days prior to sale; published in local newspaper for 3 weeks prior to sale; counties with a city of greater than 50,000 residents require published notice for 20 days (with last day on date of sale); other counties require published notice weekly for 4 consecutive weeks, with final notice no more than 7 days prior to sale.

Redemption period requirements: Borrower must declare intent with lender at least 10 days prior to sale. Borrower must post bond within 20 days after the sale of all interest, costs, damages, and 6% interest and then has 12-month redemption.

Montana

Type of foreclosure process: Both.

Process period: 150 to 180 days.

Type of deed: Both.

Notice of default: None.

Notice of sale requirements: Notice to borrower at least 120 days prior to sale; posted on property at least 20 days prior to sale; published in local newspaper for 3 consecutive weeks prior to sale.

Redemption period requirements: None.

Nebraska

Type of foreclosure process: Judicial.

Process period: 120 to 180 days average.

Type of deed: Mortgage Deed.

Notice of default: Required to borrower.

Notice of sale requirements: Judicial—publication in local newspaper 4 weeks prior to sale; nonjudicial—published in local newspaper for 5 weeks prior to sale, with final notice to appear 10 to 30 days prior to sale.

Redemption period requirements: None.

Nevada

Type of foreclosure process: Both; mostly nonjudicial.

Process period: 120 to 180 days.

Type of deed: Both; mostly Deed of Trust.

Notice of default: Required to borrower.

Notice of sale requirements: Notice mailed to borrower and all lien holders prior to sale; publication in local newspaper for 3 weeks prior to sale; posted in 3 public locations at least 21 days prior to sale.

Redemption period requirements: Nonjudicial—none; judicial—12 months (rare).

New Hampshire

Type of foreclosure process: Nonjudicial.

Process period: 90 days.

Type of deed: Both.

Notice of default: 30-day payment notice.

Notice of sale requirements: Notice to borrower at least 26 days prior to sale; publication in local newspaper for 3 weeks prior to sale; first notice at least 21 days before sale.

Redemption period requirements: Nonjudicial—none; judicial—12 months (rare).

New Jersey

Type of foreclosure process: Judicial.

Process period: 90 to 270 days.

Type of deed: Mortgage Deed.

Notice of default: Notice to borrower at least 30 days prior to initiation of foreclosure.

Notice of sale requirements: Notice to borrower at least 10 days prior to sale; posting on property and county courthouse; published in two local newspapers (one of which has to be largest in county).

Redemption period requirements: 10 days.

New Mexico

Type of foreclosure process: Judicial.

Process period: 120 days.

Type of deed: Mortgage Deed.

Notice of default: None.

Notice of sale requirements: Publication in local newspaper for 4 consecutive weeks, with final notice at least 3 days prior to sale.

Redemption period requirements: 9 months.

New York

Type of foreclosure process: Both; mostly judicial.

Process period: 210 to 450 days.

Type of deed: Both.

Notice of default: None.

Notice of sale requirements: Publication in local newspaper for 4 weeks.

Redemption period requirements: None.

North Carolina

Type of foreclosure process: Both; mostly nonjudicial.

Process period: 90 to 120 days.

Type of deed: Both.

Notice of default: Required to borrower.

Notice of sale requirements: Posted at county courthouse at least 20 days prior to sale; notice mailed to borrower at least 20 days prior to sale; published in local newspaper for 2 weeks.

Redemption period requirements: 10 days.

North Dakota

Type of foreclosure process: Judicial.

Process period: 90 to 150 days.

Type of deed: Mortgage Deed.

Notice of default: 30-day notice of intent.

Notice of sale requirements: Notice to borrower; published in local newspaper or legal news for 2 months, with last notice appearing at least 10 days prior to sale.

Redemption period requirements: 180 to 365 days.

Ohio

Type of foreclosure process: Judicial.

Process period: 150 to 210 days.

Type of deed: Mortgage Deed.

Notice of default: Required to borrower.

Notice of sale requirements: Published in local newspaper for 3 weeks prior to sale.

Redemption period requirements: None.

Oklahoma

Type of foreclosure process: Both.

Process period: 90 to 210 days.

Type of deed: Both.

Notice of default: Required to borrower.

Notice of sale requirements: Notice published in local newspaper for 4 consecutive weeks, with first notice at least 30 days prior to sale; recorded in county office.

Redemption period requirements: None.

Oregon

Type of foreclosure process: Both.

Process period: 150 to 180 days.

Type of deed: Both.

Notice of default: Required—4 months prior to sale.

Notice of sale requirements: Publication in local newspaper for 4 weeks, with last notice at least 20 days prior to sale.

Redemption period requirements: Nonjudicial—none; judicial—180 days.

Pennsylvania

Type of foreclosure process: Judicial.

Process period: 90 to 270 days.

Type of deed: Mortgage Deed.

Notice of default: 4 months prior to sale.

Notice of sale requirements: Notice to borrower; posted on property at least 30 days prior to sale; published in local newspaper for 3 consecutive weeks.

Redemption period requirements: None.

Rhode Island

Type of foreclosure process: Both; mostly nonjudicial.

Process period: 90 to 270 days.

Type of deed: Mortgage Deed.

Notice of default: None.

Notice of sale requirements: Notice to borrower at least 20 days prior to public notice; publication in local newspaper and legal newspaper for 3 weeks, with first notice at least 21 days prior to sale.

Redemption period requirements: None.

South Carolina

Type of foreclosure process: Judicial.

Process period: 150 to 180 days.

Type of deed: Mortgage Deed.

Notice of default: None.

Notice of sale requirements: Posted at county courthouse; published in local and legal newspapers for 3 weeks prior to sale.

Redemption period requirements: 30 days with deficiency judgment; none, if waived by lender.

South Dakota

Type of foreclosure process: Both; mostly judicial.

Process period: 90 to 150 days.

Type of deed: Both.

Notice of default: None.

Notice of sale requirements: Notice to borrower and lien holders at least 21 days prior to sale; published in local newspaper for 3 weeks prior to sale.

Redemption period requirements: 60 to 120 days.

Tennessee

Type of foreclosure process: Both; mostly nonjudicial.

Process period: 60 days.

Type of deed: Both.

Notice of default: None.

Notice of sale requirements: Published in local newspaper 3 times, with first notice at least 20 days prior to sale.

Redemption period requirements: Usually none; can be up to 720 days.

Texas

Type of foreclosure process: Both; mostly nonjudicial.

Process period: 30 to 90 days.

Type of deed: Both.

Notice of default: Required to borrower.

Notice of sale requirements: Notice mailed to borrower at least 21 days prior to sale; posted at county courthouse and filed with clerk at least 21 days prior to sale.

Redemption period requirements: None.

Utah

Type of foreclosure process: Both; mostly nonjudicial.

Process period: 150 days.

Type of deed: Both.

Notice of default: Required to borrower.

Notice of sale requirements: Posted on property and in country recorder's office at least 20 days prior to sale; published in local newspaper for 3 consecutive weeks, with final notice between 10 and 30 days prior to sale.

Redemption period requirements: Nonjudicial—none; judicial—court mandated.

Vermont

Type of foreclosure process: Both.

Process period: 90 to 270 days.

Type of deed: Both.

Notice of default: Required to borrower.

Notice of sale requirements: Notice to borrower at least 60 days prior to sale; published in local newspaper for 3 weeks, with first notice at least 21 days prior to sale.

Redemption period requirements: 180 to 365 days.

Virginia

Type of foreclosure process: Both; mostly nonjudicial.

Process period: 60 days.

Type of deed: Both.

Notice of default: Required to borrower.

Notice of sale requirements: Notice to borrower at least 14 days prior to sale.

Redemption period requirements: None.

Washington

Type of foreclosure process: Both; mostly nonjudicial.

Process period: 120 days average.

Type of deed: Both.

Notice of default: Required to borrower.

Notice of sale requirements: Must be recorded at county a minimum of 90 days prior to sale; notice to borrower and all lien holders; published in local newspaper at least once between 28th and 32nd day before sale, and again between 7th and 11th day prior to sale.

Redemption period requirements: 12 months unless waived.

Washington, D.C.

Type of foreclosure process: Nonjudicial; judicial is much less common.

Process period: 30 to 60 days average.

Type of deed: Both.

Notice of default: Notice must be sent to borrower.

Notice of sale requirements: Notice must be posted according to Mortgage Deed or Deed of Trust, or advertised in local newspaper for 5 weeks prior to sale; certified mail to borrowers 30 days prior to sale; recorded with county; sent to mayor or mayoral agent and all other lien holders.

Redemption period requirements: None.

West Virginia

Type of foreclosure process: Both.

Process period: 60 to 90 days.

Type of deed: Both.

Notice of default: Required to borrower.

Notice of sale requirements: Notice to borrower and lien holders at least 20 days prior to sale; published in local newspaper for 2 weeks prior to sale.

Redemption period requirements: 20 days.

Wisconsin

Type of foreclosure process: Both; mostly judicial.

Process period: 90 to 290 days.

Type of deed: Both.

Notice of default: None.

Notice of sale requirements: Varies depending on circumstances; minimum 10 months from court ruling unless waived by all parties.

Redemption period requirements: 180 to 365 days.

Wyoming

Type of foreclosure process: Both.

Process period: 60 to 90 days.

Type of deed: Both.

Notice of default: Notice to borrower at least 10 days prior to advertising sale.

Notice of sale requirements: Published in local newspaper for 4 consecutive weeks.

Redemption period requirements: 90 to 365 days.

Index

A

Agreements, 3–4
Alabama, 172
Alaska, 172
American Society of Home
    Inspectors, 21
Amortization, of loans, 89
Appraiser, 148–149
Arizona, 172–173
Arkansas, 173
Asking price, 74
Assets, carrying, 73
Assigning contract, 25
Attorney. *See* Lawyers
Auctions, 3, 15, 33, 34–37, 37–39,
    45–46, 47–49. *See also*
    Bidding
    attendance, 106–107
    bankruptcy and, 68–70
    bidder at, 37
    buyer's panic, 109, 162
    data sheet, 170
    investors and, 108
    location of, 3, 37

B

Balloon payment, 89
Bankruptcy, 26–27, 31
    Chapter 7, 68–69
    Chapter 13, 69
    good deal from, 68–70
    property in liquidation, 69–70
    purchasing after filing for, 69
    purchasing before filing for, 69
    types of, 68–69
Banks, 2, 31, 46
    purchasing REO properties
        from, 94
Bidding, 11, 37. *See also* Auctions
    high *vs.* low, 108–110
    outbidding, 162–163
    pattern of, 81
    strategies, 80–82
    "upset price," 38
Board of Realtors, 20
Borrowers:
    lenders and, 90–91
    net worth of, 91, 132
Broom clean, 54

Building-code requirements, 125
Buy-and-hold strategy, 13
Buyer's panic, 109, 162

C

California, 173
Capital gains, 133
Cash, 28
 access to, 87–90
 control of, 22
 for the homeowner, 116
 to purchase a foreclosure, 10–11
 risks and, 93–94
Cashier's check, 10, 38
Census Bureau, 6
Certified check, 39
Chain of title, 111
Chapter 7 bankruptcy, 68–69
Chapter 13 bankruptcy, 69
Checks:
 cashier's, 10, 38
 certified, 39
Closing costs, 11, 45, 89, 156
Collateral, 11
Colorado, 173–174
Commissions, 16–17
 real estate, 45
Comparables (comps), 17, 19, 43, 44, 146, 159
Connecticut, 174
Consumer debt, 6–7
Contractors, 15, 19, 21–22
 general, 21
 retired, 21
 subcontractors, 21

Contracts, assigning, 25
Cost of living, 8
Cost of sale, 45
Costs. *See also* Renovations; Repairs
 closing, 11, 45, 89, 156
 fix-up, 77–80
 money pit, 145
 opportunity, 79–80
Courthouse auctions, 47–49
Courts, 2
 issuance of a stay, 31–32
Covenant, defined, 2
Creditors, 27

D

Death, 8
Debt, 28
 consumer, 6–7
 repayment, 2
 unsecured, 32
Debtor, 3
Decision making, 64
Deed, 3, 171
Deferred payment plan, 3
Delaware, 174
Department of Housing and Urban Development (HUD), 70, 71–72, 100
Depositors, 2
Divorce, 8
"Donald, The." *See* Trump, Donald
Down payment, 39
Due diligence, 42
Dumpster, 115

E

Economic downturns, 5–7
Economics, realities of, 12
Emergencies, 6–7
Emotions, 64, 163
Equity, 28, 36
  defined, 95
Escrow accounts, 8
Eviction, 3, 4, 115–116

F

Fair market value, 12, 35, 42–45,
  44, 59. *See also* Market value;
  Properties
Fairness, sense of, 5
FDIC. *See* Federal Deposit
  Insurance Corporation
Federal Deposit Insurance
  Corporation (FDIC), 71
FHA financing, 94–95
Filing papers, 4
Financing, 87–102. *See also*
  Lenders; Loans; Walk-away
  price
  refinancing, 96
  securing, 1
Fix-up costs, 77–80
Flipping, 15, 17, 26, 59, 80,
  132–134, 155–156
Florida, 174
Forbearance plan, 153–154
Foreclosures. *See also* Profits
  action, 4
  analyzing the deal, 63–86
  avoidance of, 30

avoiding disaster, 141–164
buying as a personal residence,
  133
cancellation of sale, 31–32
commercial services for, 9
evaluation of purchase, 30
experts and, 85–86
facing, 151
financial difficulty and,
  150–155
financing the property, 87–102
good deals, 42–45
home inventory and, 11–13
homeowner irresponsibility,
  7–9
insiders, 9–10
knowledge about, 15–16
notice of, 9, 15, 33–34, 42
pre-foreclosure, 4–5, 20, 27, 28,
  29, 31, 32, 34, 36, 143
procedure for publication, 4
process of, 2, 20, 24–26, 171
public process of, 9
rates of, 5–6, 7, 8
researching, 141–142
resources, 165–166
securing the property, 103–117
stages of, 3–4
state guidelines, 171–187
success of, 15, 19
time management and, 13–14
walk-away price, 10, 12, 14
worst-case scenario, 144
Fuel costs, 8
Funding. *See* Financing; Mortgage

G

Georgia, 175
Government agencies, 70–73
Government real-estate-owned
  properties, 70–73

H

Hard money, 88
Hawaii, 175
Health problems, 8
Holding costs, 44, 80, 127, 133,
  144–145
Home equity line of credit, 96–97
Home equity loan, 95–97, 96
  advances, 6
  types of, 96–97
Home improvement loans, 4
Home improvements, 44–45
Home inspection, 56–58, 142–143
  checklist, 168–169
Home inspector, 19, 20–21, 43
  evaluation criteria, 20–21
Homeowners, 3, 27–29
  empathy toward, 5
  eviction of, 115–116
  helping, 115–116, 138
  treatment of, 137–139
  trusting, 149–150
  vacating the property, 114–116
Homes. *See also* Properties
  appreciation of, 7
  equity, 28
  fair market value, 12, 35, 42–45,
    44, 59
  inventory of, 11–13

market value of, 26, 67
move-in condition of, 53–55
visual inspection of, 43
Homes for Sale by the U.S.
  Government, 71
HUD. *See* Department of Housing
  and Urban Development

I

Idaho, 175
Illinois, 175–176
Income capitalization, 147–149.
  See also Profits
Income evaluation, 152
Indiana, 176
Insurance, 2, 11, 24–25, 54. *See
  also* Title insurance
  after possession of the property,
    104, 116–117
  back, 113–114
  premiums, 8
Interest, 87–90, 98
Internal Revenue Service (IRS),
  71
Investments, 41
  as business, 15
Investors, 2, 17, 25–26, 36
  at auctions, 108
  day job and, 161–162
  first-time, 163–164
  researching a foreclosure,
    141–142
  secret to earning profits, 1
Iowa, 176
IRS. *See* Internal Revenue Service

J
Jobs, loss of, 6–7, 8
Judgment, 2, 3, 4, 35
  money, 4
Judicial foreclosure, 24
Junior liens, 28, 60, 110
  holder of, 39
Junior obligations, 4
Jurisdiction, 4

K
Kansas, 176–177
Kentucky, 34, 177
Knowledge, 65

L
Laws, 4
Lawyers, 2, 19, 20. *See also*
  Receiver
  in bankruptcy proceedings, 26
Leasing, 7, 13
Lenders, 15, 19, 31. *See also*
  Financing
  borrowers and, 90–91
  consent of, 2
  good deals from, 73–76, 91–93
  responsibility of, 38
  standards for, 6
Letter of Credit, 11
Liber, 42
Lien, 4, 28–29, 45–46. *See also*
  Judgment
Lifestyle, 8
Limited liability corporation
  (LLC), 94

Liquidation, 69–70
Listing price, 130
LLC. *See* Limited liability
  corporation
Loans. *See also* Financing; Home
  equity loan
  amortization, 89
  assuming, 97–99
  balloon payment, 89
  collateral for, 11
  default of, 7–8
  home improvement, 4
  interest on, 87–90
  payments, 11
  preapproval, 91–92
  prepayment penalties, 89
  prequalification, 91
Loan-to-value (LTV), 89, 100
Louisiana, 177
LTV. *See* Loan-to-value

M
Maine, 177
Market value, 26, 67, 82–85. *See
  also* Fair market value
Maryland, 177–178
Massachusetts, 178
MBA. *See* Mortgage Brokers
  Association
Medical costs, unexpected, 6–7
Michigan, 24, 64, 157, 178
Minnesota, 178
Misfortune, 1–5
Mississippi, 179
Missouri, 179

Moisture damage, 143
Money. *See* Cash
Montana, 179
Mortgage, 43. *See also* Funding
  bringing it current, 152–154
  forbearance plan, 153–154
  funding for, 1
  interest rate, 98
  modification of terms of, 153
  refinancing, 96
  reinstating, 1–2
  second, 4
Mortgage broker, 19–20
Mortgage Brokers Association
  (MBA), 19
Mortgage Myths (Roberts/
  Cummings), 11, 15, 95
Moving van, 115

N
NAMB. *See* National Association
  of Mortgage Brokers
National Association of Mortgage
  Brokers (NAMB), 19
Nebraska, 180
Negotiations, 3–4, 76
Neighborhoods, 43
  bad, 5–7
  "do-wanner," 84–85
  familiarity with, 51–52
  researching, 63–65
Net worth, 91, 132
Nevada, 180
New Hampshire, 180
New Jersey, 180–181
New Mexico, 181

New York, 181
NOD. *See* Notice of default
Nonperforming investment, 157
Nonredemption certificate, 105
North Carolina, 181
North Dakota, 182
Note, 43
Notice of default (NOD), 9, 33–34,
  171
Notice of sale requirements, 171

O
Ocwen, 71
Offers, 49
  blanket, 76
  initial, 74
  multiple, 75–76
  on multiple properties, 76
  single, 74–75
Ohio, 182
Oklahoma, 182
OPM. *See* Other people's money
Opportunity, 63–65
  cost of, 79–80
  running out of time, 65
  wasting time, 65–66
Oregon, 182–183
Other people's money (OPM), 11,
  93

P
Partnerships, 13–14, 22,
  101–102
  business arrangement, 22
Payment, default of, 2
Pennsylvania, 183

People skills, 17–18
PMI. *See* Private mortgage
   insurance
Points, 88
Predatory lending, 8
Pre-foreclosure, 4–5, 20, 27, 28,
   29, 31, 32, 34, 36, 143. *See
   also* Foreclosures
Private mortgage insurance (PMI),
   48
Profits, 41, 43, 45, 119–139,
   145–149, 158–160. *See also*
   Income capitalization
after sale of the property,
   126–127, 129–131
defined, 135–137
lack of, 128–129
from renovations, 121–125
time and, 126–127
Promissory note, 43
Properties. *See also* Fair market
   value; Home inspection;
   Homes
building-code requirements, 125
complete rehab of, 158
condemned, 64
condition of, 99–100
demand for, 159
financing, 87–102
first impression of, 131
hidden systems, 55
in liquidation, 69–70
listing, 16–17
listing price, 130
location, 82–85
maintenance of, 56

market value, 26, 67, 82–85
as money pit, 145
owners vacating, 114–116
repaired value, 20
sale of, 129–131
sale of, during the renovation
   stage, 134–135
searching for, 41–61
securing, 103–117
structural issues, 55–56, 143
taking possession of, 103–106
value of, 1, 58–60, 80–82, 147,
   165–166
vandalism/theft, 104
Property taxes, 8, 24–25
after possession of the property,
   104
lien on, 46
Property worksheet, 43
Public sale, 3
Purchase price, 77–80

R
Real estate agents, 15, 16–19,
   32–33, 50–51
buyer's agent, 16
commission to, 45
evaluation of, 17
experience of, 18
good deal through, 66–68
good *vs.* bad, 17
listing agent, 16
marketing and, 130
people skills, 17–18
qualities of, 17
seller's agent, 16

Real-estate-owned (REO)
    properties, 18–19, 32, 33,
    47–49
    purchasing from banks, 94
Receiver, 2, 3, 35, 36, 68
Redemption period, 24, 26, 103,
    105–106, 157, 171
Referee, 36
Refinancing, 96
    cash-out, 6
Register of Deeds, 9, 42, 43
REITs, 88
Renovations, 11, 25, 131, 158
    costs of, 159–160
    profits from, 121–125
    before the sale, 119–121
    unnecessary, 104–105
    value added, 159
Rental properties, 13
REO. See Real-estate-owned
    properties
Repaired value, 20
Repairs, 2, 11, 15, 25, 29, 35,
    44–45, 53–55, 130–131,
    144–145, 156–157
    after possession of the property,
    104, 126–127
Rhode Island, 183
Risks, 15
    analysis of, 12
Rules, 4

S
Sales comparison. See
    Comparables (comps)
Salvage departments, 48

Second mortgage, 4, 60–61
Senior lien, 60
Septic system, 55
Service, defined, 4
Sheriff, 115
Sheriff's deed, 3
Short sale, 28, 36, 37
Skills, 65
Small Business Administration, 71
South Carolina, 183
South Dakota, 184
States. See also individual states
    foreclosure guidelines, 171–187
    requirements, 23
Stay, defined, 31–32
Storage, 116
Surplus monies, 39

T
Taxes, 11
    back, 113–114
    capital gains, 133
    escrow accounts, 8
    property, 8, 24–25, 46, 104
Team. See Partnerships
Tennessee, 184
Texas, 184
Time, 13–14, 30–31, 63–65, 80,
    127
    doing self-repairs and upgrades,
    126–127
    saved, 156–157
Title commitment, 42, 60
Title company, 19, 21
Title insurance, 4, 110–113
    chain of title, 111, 112

Trespassing, 14, 43
Trump, Donald, 16
Trustees, 68
   court-appointed, 26
Trust officers, 2. *See also* Banks

U
Unemployment rates, 8
"Upset price," 38
U.S. Customs Seizures, 71
USDA Real Estate for Sale,
   71
Utah, 184–185
Utilities, 11

V
VA. *See* Veterans Affairs
Vandalism/theft, 104
Vermont, 185

Veterans Affairs (VA), Department
   of, 70–72
   financing, 94–95
Virginia, 185

W
Walk-away price, 10, 12, 14, 35,
   70–73
   calculation worksheet, 167
Washington state, 185
Washington, D.C., 186
Water, 143
Web sites, 165–166
Well (water system), 55
West Virginia, 186
Whiteboxing, 120–121
Wholesaling, 120
Wisconsin, 186
Wyoming, 186–187